The Old West

A Poetic Documentary

Lindell Ross

By Lindell Ross

Copyright © 2015 Lindell Ross
All rights reserved.

ISBN-10: 1514808862
ISBN-13: 978-1514808863

Printed by CreateSpace,
an Amazon.com Company

DEDICATION

To my wife Pat
for encouraging and applauding
my poetic efforts.

THANK YOU

To my daughter Linda Cogswell
for her help with graphics and much else.
To my dear friend Sid Simon
for his almost flawless proofreading.
To my daughter Shelly for many Western experiences.
And to everyone at the Powderhorn Ranch
for their positive response
to my readings of my poems
around the evening campfire.

Foreword

When was the Old West?
Let's set the calendar dates
Let's say from about eighteen-forty
Until the end of the eighteen hundreds

Where was the Old West?
Let's say west of the Mississippi River
St. Louis was the Gateway to the West
Many Missouri towns were stepping stones

Why was the Old West?
A young country was pushing hard
The country was right and wrong
The people lived and died on their own

What was the Old West?
Well, let's write a hundred poems
To describe the people and places
And the events which went on

Let's call it "The Old West"
Then let's hope the hell for the best!

Table of Contents

	Page
The Pioneers	1
The Gunfighters	17
The Robbers	29
The Lawmen	39
The Native Americans	51
The Soldiers	67
The Women	81
The Prostitutes	93
The Miners	101
The Gamblers	113
The Spanish	125
The River Boaters	133
The Freight Haulers	141
The Railroaders	149
The Old, Old West	159
The West Today	173

The Pioneers

HEADIN' WEST

We're headin' out on a western trail
Takin' our chances to succeed or fail
Outriders creakin' in the saddle
All the guns loaded for battle

Sittin' on a hard bench, holdin' the rein
Men and women and children in our train
The hunter rides alone lookin' for game
The scout is out front with his Indian name

Somewhere we figger we left Missouri behind
Where they had provisions and the people were kind
We've left behind some of our eastern habits
We're on the plains shootin' for birds and rabbits

This is the longest trip of our lives
Some are recent immigrants just arrived
We all have traveled from afar
That's how we got whar we are

Floatin' down the Ohio, we didn't quit'er
We got ourselves to a St. Louis outfitter
They told us to stock up on vittles
They said we all gotta keep full kettles

We're drinkin' coffee by the tinful
We don't have no time to be sinful
All the men are alert for an Indian attack
The wagon master, he don't cut no slack

We're eatin' the bacon and the beans
Livin' our lives by any means
We got beef jerky and the hardtack
Goin' west and never comin' back

For ourselves and our families, we want the best
So we're pushin' hard and headin' west
We know our deaths could come at any hour
But we still got a little sugar and flour

Somewhere we figger we left Missouri behind
We'll be goin' over the mountains sometime
Outriders creakin' in the saddle
All the guns loaded for battle

Headin' west!

SODBUSTERS

In Oregon's Valley of the Willamette
Pronounced so as to rhyme with dammit
One of many oaths overheard by God
As they struggled to turn over the sod

In Utah, the Mormon speech more pure
How many wives per man, nobody's sure
They broke too many plowshares to estimate
Before they learned how to irrigate

When an acre of sod had been cut
Nebraska sodbusters stacked it up for a hut
When they fell asleep in these dark places
Pieces of the roof fell into their faces

Sodbusters labored with plow, shovel, and hoe
Seeded and weeded and got their crops to grow
For the land they cleared and occupied
Young America cheered and found its stride

CATTLE DRIVE

We're ridin' for the T Bar 3
All the cowboys and me
We're fresh out of the big battle
Back in Texas punchin' cattle

We been out in the thickets and thorns
Roundin' up wild and mean longhorns
Now the cow huntin' is all done
They're all branded, and I'm strappin' on a gun

We're comin' up from Texas with a big bunch
We've got almost two thousand head to punch
We're startin' on a long cattle drive
Tryin' to keep the cows and us alive

Ridin' are trail boss and foreman, Old Joe
Monty and me, Shorty, Hop, Juan and Pedro
Drivin' the hoodlum wagon is Sarge Pegleg
Cook Meechum has his chuck wagon and keg

In our remuda we got us some good horses
Young Jimmy the wrangler's got good sources
Fifteen miles today before my hot roll I fling
Listenin' to Shorty and the night riders sing

Yesterday we had some trouble we didn't need
Meechum banged on a pan and started a stampede
The cattle bolted and ran out of single file
Monty got 'em turned toward me after awhile

Ridin' the point right now is straw boss McGee
Watchin' for redskins; water and grass hopin' to see
Today I'm eatin' a lot of dust as the drag rider
Wishin' I had me a big ole jug of Texas cider

Tomorrow we're crossin' the Red River wet
We're gonna lose quite a few cows I bet
In the Indian Territories, trouble with the tribes
Then we got bushwhackers lookin' for bribes

We're comin' up from Texas with a big bunch
We're hopin' to be in Sedalia for lunch
Then shove these critters on the St. Louis train
Drink, and yell and shoot, and raise some Cain!

CHUCK WAGON COOK

I got a barrel of water strapped
      on each side of my wagon
I can cook with it, or we can
      slake our thirst, in the dry spells

Inside, I got a barrel of beans,
      a barrel of flour
A barrel of bacon,
      a barrel of coffee

If we run out of food
      this bunch might let me live
But if I run out of coffee
      my chances ain't very good

So I got another half barrel of coffee
      hid out underneath
Along with a half barrel of flour
      'cause they sure like their flapjacks

I got a whole barrel of oats
      that can keep men and horses alive
if we hit a bad stretch of country,
      which I know we will

The only other barrel I got is salt
      So I can salt down the wild game
That our hunter and the boys
      shoot along the trail when they can

Underneath my bed I got the half barrels
      of coffee and flour hid out
And half barrels of sugar and dried corn
      and half barrels of jerky and hardtack

At the back of the wagon I got a bunch
        of little drawers and cubby holes
Where I stashed the fatback and dried peas
        and some canned and dried fruit

I got canned peaches and tomatoes
        pecans, walnuts and hazelnuts
some dried plums, grapes and apples
        I brought from St. Louie

In the tin boxes I got black pepper
        sage, cinnamon, and dried spiciness
Somebody shoots a buffalo or antelope
        I want it to taste good

WINDMILLS

Throughout the Great American Plain
There is truly not very much rain

Drilling down past two hundred feet
Before the drill and the waters meet

Four winds blow across the West
Which type of windmill catches them best?

Windmills run like a big clock
Water for the people, water for the stock

Windmills turning, turning all around
Pumping, pumping water up from the ground

Searching for the wind, catching the breeze
Thankful ranchers dropping to their knees

I'M RIDIN' THIS HORSE

I'm ridin' this horse down this trail
A horse that is not my own
A trail that I did not choose

I don't care what's up ahead
'cause everything is back behind me

I got nothin' better, or worse, to do
So I'm ridin' this horse down this trail

The sky still looks kinda blue
I'm still thinkin' about you

It didn't have to be this way
I didn't choose the time or place

It all come apart in a hurry
I didn't have no time to worry

Outlaws took my money
Bank took my ranch
Drifter took my woman
Injuns took my pony

I'm ridin' this horse down this trail
'cause I got nothin' better to do

'cause I got nothin' better to do
I'm ridin' this horse down this trail

Injuns took my pony
Drifter took my woman
Bank took my ranch
Outlaws took my money

I didn't have no time to worry
It all come apart in a hurry

I didn't choose the time or place
It didn't have to be this way

I'm still thinkin' about you
The sky still looks kinda blue

So I'm ridin' this horse down this trail
I got nothin' better, or worse, to do

'cause everything is back behind me
I don't care what's up ahead

A trail that I did not choose
A horse that is not my own
I'm ridin' this horse down this trail

'cause I got nothin' better to do

A HUNDRED MILES CLOSER
--California or Bust

Last Sunday two of the oxen dropped dead
The wagon tipped over and a wheel broke

Monday we drove through a rainstorm all day
Two horses and the wagon master drowned in the river
The canvass leaked in my face all night, soaked my bed

Tuesday my wife had a nervous breakdown
One of the kids got dysentery, and one got cholera
Uncle Joe died and Grandma got diarrhea

Wednesday I was busy swattin' mosquitos
And scratchin' flea bites and chigger bites
When the rattlesnake bit me in the crotch

Thursday the Indians attacked

Friday most of us outran the prairie fire
Got across a patch of scorchin' desert
And ran into a blizzard of snow goin' up the mountain

Saturday we ran out of food and water

But when the dawn came up this Sunday
We were a hundred miles closer to the Promised Land

THE OLD EAST

The Old West wouldn't have been the Old West
Without everybody who came from the Old East

Wyatt Earp was born in Illinois
X. Beidler in Pennsylvania at Mount Joy

Billy the Kid was born in New York state
Black Bart, there from England, did immigrate

Isaac Parker, born in Maryland, was the hanging judge
Pat Garrett was raised up in the Louisiana sludge

Laura Bullion and Kid Curry, outlaws in disgrace
Both had Kentucky as their birthplace

Heck Thomas from Georgia was all about law
Georgia-born Doc Holliday was an outlaw

If people from the Old East didn't their lives invest
The Old West wouldn't have been the Old West

THE MORMON TRAIL

Though history may tell a different tale
In Vermont, began The Mormon Trail
With the visions of a teenager, it seems
Fourteen years old when came the dreams

In his dreams the Angel Moroni appeared
And told him that for Christ's church, God feared
The church was taking everyone who lived on earth
In the wrong direction, down the wrong path

Joseph Smith was the teenager's name
And again and again the visions came
Unto him the Angel Moroni a book revealed
That the angel had written and concealed

The father of the angel was called Mormon
The book was called "The Book of Mormon"
In eighteen thirty, the book was printed and bound
The book and the beliefs fell upon fertile ground

In America it was a time of great religious desire
From Vermont, the belief spread like wildfire
Through the mountains and valleys south it seres
To the sons and daughters of the Carolina pioneers

The Ross boys began to marry the Smith girls
The Smith boys began to marry the Ross girls
Not just one at a time, but two and more
Spiritual marriage part of the Mormon lore

Later, one of them to Joseph Smith was related
And to journey west with him they were fated
Some spiritual marriages wound up in the hay
And many children were born along the way

As more and more public tolerance they did lose
For Mormon marriage practices and other views
Mormons were urged to produce many offspring
For added numbers to the flock they would bring

The movement west was to escape persecution
Joseph Smith's followers, seeking a solution
Having been driven from Ohio and Missouri, too
Coming to Illinois for a rendezvous in Nauvoo

Here, Joseph Smith was assassinated in the jail
Brigham Young then took the saints upon the trail
Westward where few people lived or nested
The Mormons wanted to be left alone, unmolested

Across Iowa and the Great Plains
Along the way, birth and death pains
The most organized of the western pioneers
Great hardships, though, and shared tears

When Brigham Young declared the trail's end
In the barrens of the Great Salt Lake and Wasatch wind
Mormons settled upon land no one wanted
Perfect home for a people weary of being taunted

From the desert temple, to God, rose a white steeple
Utah now was homeland for the Mormon people
The Ross and Smith families and other devout
Were urged to claim more land and spread out

They moved onto Western land, rough and raw
Through the years, lived and died in Idaho and Utah,
In California, Washington, Wyoming, Arizona, Oregon
Mormon dreams live on in the land of the Utes
    ...and beyond

WYATT EARP

Wyatt Earp's life in the nineteenth century
Was a recitation of old western history
As lawman and gunfighter his reputation was made
But he worked in many a different trade

As a young man in Iowa he was a farmer
Until his family packed up kit and caboodle
And headed west in a covered wagon
Which caused him to become an Indian fighter

Then he became a stagecoach driver
A wagon freighter and a railroad grader
And in one of the stranger twists
Boxing referee for men fighting with their fists

Wyatt hired on as hunter for a party of surveyors
Headed into the unexplored Indian Territories
Later he hunted for buffalo on the Plains
As did Wild Bill, Buffalo Bill, and other Bills

He broke the faro bank in the Oriental Saloon
Dealt faro and monte at the Long Branch
Tamed the wild cowboys as a lawman
Wore the badge in Wichita, Dodge, Tombstone

Hauled firewood down the hills to Deadwood
Rode shotgun on stagecoaches and the railroad
Invested in mining ventures and oil land
At the end, called himself a businessman

GATEWAY TO THE WEST

For people who wanted to head west
Missouri was first on their quest
St. Louis and several other towns
Gateways to going beyond the bounds

Lewis and Clark were the first to depart
St. Louis was where they got their start
Then trappers brought back furs and hides
Missouri River steamboats began their rides

In St. Joseph the Pony Express began
Young riders headed west fast as they can
First drive of cattle, Texas born and bred
Cowboys brought to the Sedalia railhead

In Independence many began their travails
On the Oregon, California, and Santa Fe trails
West Port too, launched many pioneers
Heading west with their hopes and fears

Rising early, before the night was done
Setting forth toward the setting sun
Leaving in the Missouri moonbeam
Heading for their western dream

The Gunfighters

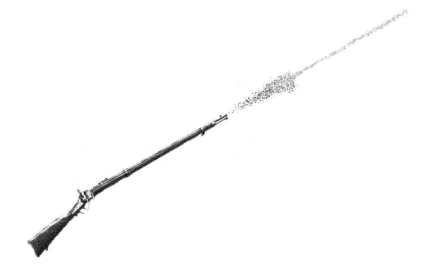

A FAMILY AFFAIR

The great thing about gunfighting in the old days
It was a family affair: the children were there
There was Billy the Kid, Kid Curry, The Apache Kid
And Fred E. Sutton, the Crooked S Kid

The great thing about gunfighting in the old days
It was a family affair: the brothers were there
There was Frank and Jesse James, Cole and Bob Younger
Sam and Black Jack Ketchum of Hole-in-the-Wall gang

The great thing about gunfighting in the old days
It was a family affair: brothers <u>and</u> cousins were there
Ike and Billy Clanton, Frank and Tom McLaury
Frank, Emmitt, and Bob Dalton; cousins of the Youngers

The great thing about gunfighting in the old days
It was a family affair on the other side of the law there
There was Morgan, Virgil, and Wyatt Earp
Ed and Bat Masterson, and the Pinkertons, too

Bullets flying through the air; it was a family affair

SHOWDOWN AT THE O.K. CORRAL

They all had a burr under their saddle
So there had to be a big gun battle
Some of these men just had to die
And every one of them knew why

Things were not okay
Before, during, or after
The showdown at the O.K. Corral
It was all very complicated

Some cowboys don't have good sense
Threatening the three Earp brothers
Was like pokin' a finger in a rattlesnake den
Keep it up and somebody's goin' to get bit

Clantons and McLaurys didn't have good sense
Of course they were part cowboy and part rustler
In fact, the Clantons stole Wyatt's race horse
Wyatt had caught Billy Clanton riding it

Time marched on by in Tombstone
Then one day Ike Clanton came to town
He drank in the saloons all night long
In the morning he felt ready to fight

"As soon as these damned Earps make their appearance
on the streets today, the ball will open."
Virgil Earp, marshal of Tombstone, saw Ike in an alley
Ike was armed, which was against the town law

Virgil took his rifle away and hit him over the head
Ike was hauled into court, lost his guns, and was fined
Afterwards, Ike threatened Morgan Earp
"I'll fight you anywhere or any way."

All the words hurled back and forth
Finally turned to flying lead
The rattle of gunfire lasted under a minute
Heavy clouds of smoke swirled over the scene

Three men lay dead or dying
Three men lay wounded on the ground
Ike Clanton had taken off running
Wyatt Earp was the only man left standing

It had started with the click, click
Of cowboys cocking their six-shooters
"Hold! I want your guns," yelled Virgil.
But they did not respond in words

Billy Clanton aimed and fired toward Wyatt
Ignoring Billy, Wyatt gut-shot Frank McLaury
The most dangerous gunman of that bunch
Billy's bullet missed Wyatt

Doc Holliday blasted Tom McLaury
With a shotgun, though he was unarmed
But then Doc was not that particular
About such details, when helping his friends

Morgan then shot and hit Billy twice
Though down, Billy hit Virgil in the calf of his leg
Frank McLaury, also down, shot Doc in the hip
Just as Morgan's shot finished Frank off

Billy Clanton, who had said earlier,
"I didn't come here to fight anyone,
and no one wants to fight me."
Fired his dying shot into Morgan's shoulder

The showdown at the O.K. Corral was over
But the shooting and killing continued
Two months later Virgil's arm was shattered
By buckshot fired from ambush

Three months later Morgan's spine was shattered
By shots fired through the glass in the back door
Of the pool hall as he leaned over the table
Morgan was dead in half an hour

Three men were seen running away
A Clanton friend, a sheriff's deputy, and a Mexican
Three days later the deputy was found dead
In Tucson, where Wyatt and Doc had just left

Wyatt formed a posse of friends
To hunt down the other two shooters
They found and killed the Mexican woodcutter
But the Clanton family friend left the area

Wyatt's posse was being pursued
By the crooked county sheriff's posse
To arrest Wyatt and Doc for the dead deputy
So they and a few friends headed to New Mexico

The showdown finally over, no more flying lead
One more wounded, three more dead
Some of these men just had to die
And every one of them knew why

ANOTHER NOTCH ON HIS GUN

Men with notches on their gun
Were pretty much crazy
Seemed to shoot people for fun

Several of them were riding around the Old West
One called himself McCarty or Bonney or Antrim
As Billy the Kid, he was known the best

But for the greatest number of men shot down
Killing forty-four with his Colt forty-five
John Wesley Hardin was the terror of the town

Clay Allison would shoot at the drop of a hat
The Confederate Army had found him unfit for duty
On various whims, he killed a lot of people after that

Bill Longley said in Dakota there was no law at all
He figured he killed thirty-two, and in his words
"Claw, tooth, fang; the weakest went to the wall."

Longley was hung for his murderous mark
Allison died accidentally under a wagon wheel
Hardin shot from behind; Billy the Kid shot in the dark

The way these bad men's deaths were done
No gunfight in the street at high noon
Nobody deserved another notch on his gun

WILD BILL

James Butler Hickok in the birth books
Wild Bill had courage and good looks
Always well-armed, with a sharpshooter's eye
Not just a myth, but a real deal guy

Wild Bill was full of skill
Bill was also full of bull
Of all the lying gunfighters traced
He was the most bald-faced

Reputation might give them an edge
Opponents might shake and hedge
Bill didn't want them to think he could lose
But the man really had paid his dues

During the Civil War, he operated behind
The enemy Confederate line
Then as a U.S. Army scout
He sought the Indians out

In Colorado, Bill rescued thirty-four men
Riding back and forth through all the Indians
As Marshal of Abilene, though, friend or foe
Found him at a poker table in the Alamo

Bill was known far and wide
There was no place he could hide
His fame became so great
He was known state-to-state

A newspaper reported Wild Bill to be
Many places in eighteen seventy-three
Killed in Galveston, fair and square
In New York, airing his long hair

Visiting in Missouri with his relations
By Omaha, killing three of the Indian Nations
Shot to death in Fort Dodge
Outside some rustic lodge

Bill's life took a sudden downward bent
When he shot his deputy by accident
He became a bum on the ramble
All he did was booze and gamble

Wild Bill was shot in the back of the head
Fell forward, aces and eights he did spread
Now, forever known as the dead man's hand
Bill was dead in Deadwood in Dakota land

PAYING THEIR RESPECTS

Top gunfighters had no desire to face each other
Lawman or outlaw, they thought like a brother
They didn't want to give their guns a try
For one or both of them would surely die

Nobody would dare to call them yeller
For thinking discretion the better part of valor
On opposite sides of the law they might be
But sometimes they acted quite friendly

Doc Holliday was known for killing lawmen
But to Wyatt Earp he was a loyal friend
He stood shoulder-to-shoulder with Wyatt
And at the O.K. Corral broke Tombstone's quiet

Wild Bill Hickok, marshal of Abilene town
With John Wesley Hardin he palled around
Hardin, the ruthless killer of forty-four men
With Wild Bill drank and whored around in sin

Then one night a sudden shot ended it all
From his hotel bed Hardin fired through the wall
The shot killed the man in the room next door
Hardin just couldn't stand the man's loud snore

Realizing what he had done, he sprang from bed
Out the window and into the night he fled
For he knew Wild Bill would come for him
And the odds of either one living would be slim

One day Frank and Jesse James rode into Abilene
They got word to Wild Bill they wouldn't do mean
But if he came for them, a message heeded by Bill
They had picked out a place for him in Boot Hill

Jesse James and Wild Bill were such great shots
Years later their assassins chose their only spots
In ultimate respect for their gunfighting skill
Shot in the back of the head the only way to kill

THE BIBLE OR THE GUN

Some folks read in the Bible of God's holy wrath
And walked on the straight and narrow path

Other folks caused a lot of death and travail
As they shot their way down the outlaw trail

These two kinds of folks were sometimes related
Though their similarities are overrated

Jesse James was a devilish creature
His father was a Baptist preacher

John Wesley Hardin a killer most sinister
His father was a Methodist minister

Butch Cassidy roosted on the robbers' perch
His grandfather was a bishop of the Mormon church

The Bible says the sins of the fathers
Shall be visited upon the sons

Apparently, the piety of the fathers
Not bestowed upon those who lived by their guns

The Robbers

BAD BOYS OF MISSOURI

Was it the drinkin' water
      bein' pumped up from the ground?
Was it the Missouri mud
      layin' all around?

Whatever the reason it might be
      There were a lot of bad boys from Missouri
Everybody knows about Jesse and Frank
      And how they liked to rob a bank

Cole Younger's father, though no bolder
      In Jackson County, a wealthy officeholder
Most of the cousins, the Dalton boys, were born
      In Cass County, and became objects of scorn

Though the Dalton boys, except one man
      Were wiped out in a bad robbery plan
Bill Doolin, their Arkansas protégé, had success
      Until the marshal's shotgun left him a mess

One of the really bad boys, so they tell
      Was a Missouri girl named Belle
Her father owned a farm, slaves, and hotel
      She bore Cole Younger a little Belle

Belle then married a Cherokee outlaw
      Sam Starr, one of the worst she saw
Later she held hands with Blue Duck
      Said any outlaw was welcome to her luck

Kid Curry lived with his aunt in Dodson
      Until a teenager, when he picked up a gun
Tom Horn grew up on a farm in Memphis, Mo.
      Shot people for money, high and low

    The bad boys of Missouri were a tough crowd
          The noise from their guns was loud
Not all the boys of Missouri were bad
          But some were the worst we ever had

ME AND JESSE

Jesse James was born in Missouri
And so the hell was I
But we don't see eye-to-eye

Jesse was a Confederate guerilla
Slaughtering without precedents
Covered with the blood of innocents

A hundred years later
Two hundred miles further south
I speak with a Union mouth

Jesse, I always wondered
My words comin' with a Southern drawl
What the hell was the matter with y'all?

JESSE JAMES' WAR

Confederate soldiers were given amnesty
Confederate guerillas were not so lucky
Those who fought with Anderson and Quantrill
Were treated as enemies still

Frank James turned himself in
And was paroled by the Northern army men
Jesse was carrying a white flag of surrender
When he was shot by a Northern offender

The sheriff had him taken home to die
But he lived to spit in their eye
Perhaps thinking about their unfair games
So began the <u>un</u>civil war of Jesse James

He got a gang of former guerillas together
Men of guns and horses and leather
Banks, trains, stagecoaches they robbed
Like guerilla raids, they pulled their jobs

Like Quantrill and Bloody Bill from the past
They did thorough planning, hit hard and fast
They used the tactics they had been taught
Shoot straight, fade away and don't get caught

The number and identities of gang members
Ebbed and flowed like glowing embers
Besides Jesse and Frank, the Younger brothers
Cole, Bob, Jim, and John, plus many others

Some gang members were shot and killed
And many of their victims' lives were stilled
And townspeople who fought back
Died in Jesse James' warlike attack

Jesse was always a Confederate in belief
Shooting him in surrender brought many grief
He knew what had been done to family and friend
And they knew what had been done to him

Order Number Eleven had been inhumane
Upon the Union Army, an awful stain
To vacate their homes, which were burned
Innocents killed, same as the guerillas they spurned

So Jesse had the support of the rural folks
In Missouri and many states, his name invoked
If Jesse wanted to keep fighting his war
It gave them something to cheer for

Farmers needing loans, the banks they did hate
Because of tight credit and high interest rate
The other people that Jesse robbed
Were not ones with whom they hobnobbed

Jesse James' war lasted fifteen long years
Three times longer than the Civil War tears
They robbed for money, but with such hostility
Maybe reacting to much Northern incivility

KID CURRY BREAKS EVEN

Kid Curry was a cowboy
He could rope and ride
Break the toughest bronc
Skin out the toughest hide

Kid Curry was a traveler
He traveled far and wide
From the mountains of Montana
To the hills of Tennessee he did hide

Kid Curry was a lover
Meg was a wild Mormon wife
The girls of Paris a true delight
Annie Rogers the love of his life

Kid Curry was a killer
He killed for revenge
He killed in self defense
But never went on a killing binge

Kid Curry was a friend
Often he rode with the Wild Bunch
Butch Cassidy and the Sundance Kid
Often asked for his best hunch

Kid Curry was a robber
He robbed trains and banks
He stole horses and gold
And he never said thanks

Kid Curry was a prisoner
A year in the Knoxville jail
Then he got ahold of a gun
Lit out on a westward trail

Kid Curry was a loving brother
John and Lonnie and Lou
Hank and Bob and Alice
To all of them, he was true

Kid Curry was a victim
Mean, bungling officers of the law
Mistreated his family so badly
It always stuck in his craw

Kid Curry was an orphan
His mother died of a disease
His father ran away with a woman
He had no childhood of ease

Kid Curry was a cowboy
A victim, friend, and a lover
An outlaw, thief, and a killer
An orphan, a man, and a brother

Kid Curry was a tough man
Though he never was a hero
Add up his pluses and minuses
He might be happy with a zero

THEY PULLED THE SHADES DOWN

As I rode out of their town
They pulled all of the shades down

The deed that I had done
Didn't really help anyone

I robbed their little bank
For that, they have me to thank

Not in the land of milk and honey
I rode away with all their money

At the very edge of that town
I dropped the bank bag on the ground

The first time I ever give up my loot
Since I first become a real owlhoot

LAST GANG IN THE OLD WEST

Eighteen sixty-six was the year
In which Jesse James began his career
Leaving behind the war against the Yank
Jesse raided his first Missouri bank

In that same year, early one morn
Baby Robert LeRoy Parker was born
As was Jesse, he was born of religious kin
Grandson of a Mormon bishop, without sin

Later he chose the name Butch Cassidy
Led the Wild Bunch in their audacity
They robbed banks and trains
Rustled horses and cattle for ill-gotten gains

Among his gang, Harry Longabaugh hid
He was better known as the Sundance Kid
Ben Kilpatrick, "The Tall Texan," was in love
With Laura Bullion, a soiled dove

Harvey Logan was also a mainstay
He was known as Kid Curry in his heyday
Perhaps the deadliest of the whole lot
For revenge and self-defense, men he shot

Gang members came and went sporadically
Butch ran his gang democratically
Members were welcome to give their input
Butch was not one to put down his foot

Though some of his gang shot people dead
"I have never killed a man," Butch said
When the law was in hot pursuit
Not at men, but at horses he did shoot

In a phrase that now sounds laughable
Wanted posters said he was "cheery and affable."
And finally, the Pinkertons were closing in
The Union Pacific sent a train full of armed men

So Butch, Sundance, the Kid's mistress Etta Place
In nineteen oh-one, journeyed to an eastern base
They toured all of New York City, except the jail
Then for South America, they did set sail

The Lawmen

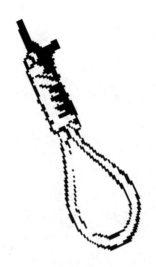

LYNCH LAW

In Bedford County, Virginia during the Revolution
Law and order was quite an absent institution
Then a justice of the peace, without a big speech
Threw himself right into the legal breach

Charles Lynch ruled from the bench
He didn't give the damn crooks an inch
With no jail, he dealt out whippings and fines
Hanged the Tories who tried to blow up lead mines

Later on an official investigation recommended
That this unofficial judge was to be commended
Later still this man's good name came into misuse
To mean hanging without a trial or proper excuse

In the California gold rush, lynching was the name
For hanging a man accused of jumping a claim
In the Old West stealing a horse or a cow
Could get the rustler strung from the nearest bough

The worst perversion of Lynch's name
Was our country's Southern racial shame
For over fifty years, Blacks old and young
For crimes real or imagined were hung

Charles Lynch was a courageous man so rare
Using his name for lynchings is not fair
Law judged by Charles Lynch was sound and good
"Lynch law" he would not have understood

THE HANGING JUDGE

Now Oklahoma; then Indian Territories
The Indians were given it all
But white men again came to call

It was refuge for the worst of the worst
The James boys liked to vacation there
The Daltons killed and gave everybody a scare

The position of judge had been vacant
Nobody wanted the impossible task
Isaac Parker took it; nobody had to ask

He was appointed by President Grant
Parker had been city attorney in St. Joe
And a two-term Congressman, you know

He had the best of motivations
Wanting to help the Five Civilized Tribes
Oppose evil, and take no bribes

Leaving the comfort of Missouri behind
He moved to Fort Smith, Arkansas
Where they badly needed some kind of law

Western Arkansas and the Indian Territories
Seventy thousand square miles of jurisdiction
Appointed as judge without restriction

His rulings were not subject to review
By any other court in the land
Because crime was so out-of-hand

The President also appointed a U.S. Marshal
And two hundred deputies he did hire
Because the situation was so dire

Though tears rolled down his cheek
Judge Parker's gavel came down with a bang
As he sentenced six men to hang

Thousands came from miles around
It was big news coast-to-coast
He became "The Hanging Judge," without a boast

Judge Parker got the job done
He always had a full docket
Never put money in his pocket

As the years passed on by
He sentenced one hundred sixty men to die
The Executioner hung sixty of them high

With all the criminals riding around
What should two hundred deputies do?
Bring in only a token few?

With more than thirteen thousand cases
In over twenty years on the bench
Only eight men a year to legally lynch

Brutal crooks, rapists, and killers
Sentenced to the noose
But some wanted to turn them loose

Those safely in the East
The U.S. Supreme Court
Lawyers who distort

In later years the judge came under attack
In a shrinking territory, he still held sway
But his rulings were overturned day-by-day

Many of the lawless were set free
Judge Parker dealt with Western realities
His opponents fed upon Eastern technicalities

Parker did an outstanding job
Unfortunately, in the end
He was judged by lesser men

Instead of the reward he deserved
For judging those who had sinned
"The Hanging Judge" was left twisting in the wind

HEAD GAMES

Wyatt Earp was a smart son-of-a-bitch
To pull a quick trigger he had no itch
With a thousand cowboys camped outside of town
If he shot one, the rest would gun him down

So his way of dealing with a cowboy who was drunk
Was to hit him on the head with a clunk
On the side of the head with his pistol barrel
Couldn't hit him on top because of his sombrero

Then he would help the cowboy upright
And take him off to jail for the night
Next morning when the court held session
He would be fined a hundred dollars for indiscretion

The cowboy rode back out to the camp
The cowboys laughed at the dumb scamp
The marshal lived to fight another day
That was Wyatt Earp's clever way

Bat Masterson was a good friend of Wyatt
Bat also knew how to prevent a riot
Some say Bat was short for Bartholemew
Others noted the cane with which he could hit you

Bat was a sheriff who dressed so dapper
With his cane he gave the accused a tapper
Like Wyatt, he was good with a gun
But chose to smack the side of the head a good one

Wyatt's brother Virgil, also a lawman
Knew it was better with a clout to command
Than to try to rule with flying lead
Which could get you a bullet in the head

These men successfully enforced the law
They didn't want to put a bullet in your craw
They chose to use a minimum of force
But everybody knew they could shoot you, of course

COWTOWNS OF KANSAS

Abilene, Wichita, Hays, Ellsworth
    Dodge City—the Kansas towns!
Thousands of head of cattle
    to put on the trains.
Hundreds of cowboys
    camped outside of town.

This was all just after the Civil War
    Texas had been a Confederate state
Maybe Texans still had a lot of hate
    They sure didn't respect the townspeople
Maybe saw them as damn Yankees
    A free state true to the Union

Plus the cowboys had just come off
    A long, hard trail
Got the job done, got their pay
    Wanted to raise some hell
Drink and gamble and shoot
    And chase some quail

The rowdiest ones got smacked
    Up aside the head
Spent the night in jail
    Were fined a hundred dollars
By the judge in the morning
    Rode out of town partly sober

If a lawman shot and killed one
        Hundreds more might ride into town
Shoot it up some more
        And kill the lawmen dead
So to keep the peace
        Lawmen just knocked'em in the head

Wyatt Earp was always thinkin'
        A lightning fast man with a gun
But he let the cowboys live
        He was a prairie sage
Just hit'em in the head with the barrel
        Wyatt lived to a ripe old age

Wyatt Earp, Wild Bill Hickok, Bill Tilghman
        And a lot of other marshals and sheriffs
Put them all in their rightful place
        Tried to limit their disgrace
Ed Masterson tried to talk some sense into them
        They shot him; brother Bat took over then

Cowboys will be cowboys
        And Texans will be Texans
They still make some noise today
        When they come up north
In the good old summertime
        To cool down, drink, and play

SWITCHING SIDES

There was a line drawn in the sand
On one side, the scoundrels of outlaw land
On the other side of the border
The forces of law and order

>Many ignored the sign
>Crossed over that line
>From lawman to outlaw
>From outlaw to lawman

In Ada County, Idaho the sheriff came to grief
They strung him up for being a horse thief
Citizens of Laramie, Wyoming were impartial
For drugging and robbing, hung the town marshal

>Down in New Mexico, Henry Brown's courses
>Were killing lawmen and stealing horses
>But Caldwell, Kansas needed a lawman bad
>He turned out to be the best they ever had

They gave him a new rifle from the town
Henry married a local girl, settled down
Suddenly, one day he tried a bank to rob
Over in Medicine Lodge, got shot by a mob

>Ben Thompson was a ruthless gunman
>The people of Austin, Texas hired him
>To be town marshal, and thought he was great
>Until he shot an old enemy downstate

One time two of the Dalton brother dears
Took time out of their criminal careers
Gave desperadoes in Indian Territories a nudge
And testified before the Hanging Judge

                In Dallas, Texas for two years, no mistake
                Cole, Bob, and Jim Younger took a break
                Helped the sheriff bring crooks before the bar
                And sang in the Baptist church choir

Some towns hired outlaws to do the law stuff
Because they were the only ones tough enough
One druggist worked out very well
But some shopkeepers got blown to hell

                Switching sides was common on the range
                Some lawmen and outlaws never did change
                But with all that switching back sides
                You sure had to watch your backsides

The Native Americans

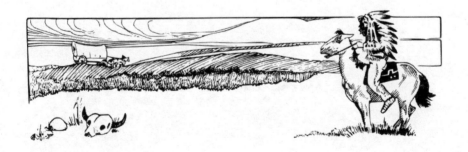

INDIAN NAMES

There was One Bull and Tall Bull
But the bull with the most pull
Was the Sioux Chief Sitting Bull

There was American Horse and White Horse
But the horse with the biggest force
Was the Sioux Chief Crazy Horse

There was White Bear and Yellow Bear
Swift Bear and Kicking Bear, an active pair
Sitting Bull's bodyguard, Catch-the-Bear

Sitting Bull was killed by Red Tomahawk
Who appeared to have a serious squawk
But killed with a bullet, not a tomahawk

There was White Bird and Red Wing
Some names that have a nice ring
There was Crow King and Iron Wing

Spotted Tail and Black Prairie Chicken
Rain-in-the-Face, names I wouldn't be pickin'
Did I mention Eat Dog and Black Prairie Chicken?

TRADING POST

For several tribes Fort Laramie was their trading post
For southern plains tribes Taos was their host

For plains Indians trading was a way of life
Whether for a horse, a gun, a kettle, or a knife

Comanche, Kiowa, Arapaho, and Cheyenne
Traded with each other, and with the white man

They might offer a robe of buffalo
For a yard and a half of calico

Or thirty, thick beaver's pelt
For a keg of rum might be dealt

Or they might trade a horse to ride
For a total of ten weasel's hide

But a horse that with lightning speed runs
Could be traded for ten guns

Five buffalo robes wouldn't be reckless
If traded for a genuine bear-claw necklace

And some goods the Spaniards always gave
In exchange for an unfortunate Indian slave

ANIMAL SPIRITS

There is power in the spirits of the animals
We call upon these spirits for favor

The skunk has many supernatural powers
The blood of the badger foretells our future

The spirits of the hawk and the eagle
Go with us when we ride the path of war

The bull elk calls a mate when he bugles
His spirit can help in matters of love

The bear is hard to kill, healing himself
So we seek for his spirit to heal us

The rattlesnake has power to bring rain
Down to the dry ground where he lives

The beaver is called the little buffalo
And to us he is the symbol of food

The cricket, horned toad, and raven
Show us the direction to the buffalo herd

The spirits of all these animals
Help us in the struggles we face every day

SONG OF A WARRIOR

My song rises to the mountain tops
My song drifts to the desert sands
I have bowed to the four winds that blow

I have sought favor of the one who is above
I have sought favor of the one who is here below
My spirit is joined with all the spirits around me

I am armed with the spirit and claw of the eagle
I am armed with the spirit and beak of the hawk
I shall count coup in the camp of my enemies

My arrows shall fly straight and true
My tomahawk shall find its mark
My knife shall cut quickly and cleanly

I shall return with scalps on my belt
I shall return with horses for my people
I shall count coup in the camp of my enemies

MEDICINE MAN

From his dream, the medicine man drew his power
Now he leads the chants, hour after hour

He makes his deerskin rattle dance
As he keeps the tempo for the tribal chants

When his medicine bundle is unrolled
Objects inside have sacred value untold

He can foresee the future, once unknown
He can heal the sick, flesh and bone

We wonder, and feel his solemn stare
As he waves his painted dolls in the air

He does detailed paintings in the sand
Places the four directions under his command

At finding what is lost, he does amazingly well
And upon the unsuspecting, casts a love spell

He knows all the plants and the cures
He will be revered as long as his magic endures

He can make the weather fair or foul
But if he violates a taboo, he can only howl

He is our trusted tribal medicine man
He does what nobody else in the tribe can

TRIBAL MATCHMAKER

The Chickasaw chick
     and the Iroquois boy.
The Walla Walla woman
     and the Mandan man.
The Wichita woman
     and the Yuma man.
The Wappo woman
     and the Cheyenne man.

I have a Havasupai papa
     and a Miami momma.
A Quapaw pa
     and a Chocktaw ma.
A Hopi poppy
     and a Menominnee mommy.
A Papago papa
     and a Washo momma.

What if a Flathead woman
     married a Blackfoot man?
What would the kids look like?
     A black head and flat feet?

What if a Kickapoo man
     married a Potawatomi woman?
Would the baby be a Kickawatomi?
     Or a Potapoo?

Oh, the tribal matchmaker:
If he don't have'er,
I won't take'er!

INDIAN WOMEN

To provide food, clothing, and shelter
Indian women worked helter-skelter
They taught their children how to behave
Tribal ways for the woman and young brave

While the men hunted for meat
Women gathered wild plants to eat
They gathered nuts and fruits
They gathered vegetables and roots

Then they gathered bundles of firewood
And cooked everything up to taste good
They dried strips of meat for trail rations
And decorated food pouches in tribal fashions

Indian women staked and scraped animal skin
Then cut and sewed clothes for all their kin
They decorated with fringes and quills
Wove baskets, bending the grass to their wills

Women sewed together buffalo hides
To cover their tipi on all sides
They put it up around the tall poles
Then they double-checked it for holes

Indian women of the western plains
For children and home life held the reins
Women who were native to this land
Mirrored the work of the white woman's hand

TRAIL OF TEARS
--Red, White, & Blue

It was a time of dark days and evil nights
A terrible stain upon the fabric of our nation
The way Native Americans were treated by whites
Was the way Nazis treated the Jewish population

The Cherokee people were among those harmed
In 1829, in the state of Georgia, where it began
Where the Cherokee peacefully, successfully farmed
The state wanted white people to have the Cherokee land

Peacefully, the Cherokee sought legal interdiction
Hoping against hope, the rulings would be impartial
The Supreme Court ruled Indians a federal jurisdiction
Not the states, said Chief Justice John Marshall

But President Andrew Jackson made smart aleck sounds
"He has made his decision, now let him enforce it."
This shirking of duty would seem impeachment grounds
Whites clung to "Manifest Destiny," and wouldn't quit

Government policy was to displace Indians, from 1800 on
In the southeast the "Five Civilized Tribes" the goals
The Indian Removal Act of 1830 to make them gone
The Cherokee, Chickasaw, Choctaw, Creek, Seminoles

General Scott and seven thousand soldiers or more
Acting under President Jackson's authorities
Forced the Cherokee from their homes, door-to-door
Oklahoma was the destination, the Indian Territories

It was the winter of eighteen thirty-eight and nine
No time to prepare given to families of Cherokee
No time, no belongings, no respect, get in line
From Georgia, Alabama, North Carolina, Tennessee

Of the 17,000 men, women, and children, the disclosure
Of those forced on the 1,500 mile trip by army gunners
Almost half died of disease, malnutrition, and exposure
Of the Bataan Death March, one of the forerunners

Blood and tear stains in the dark Cherokee night
A stain upon all the white Americans, too
For our American flag, a red stain upon the white
About which all Americans should feel very blue

TREATIES WITH THE INDIANS
--Two Different Treatments

In America
    For treaties it was white government dictation
    There was not the normal two-party negotiation
    To the Indians the terms were not even made clear
    Whites broke and re-wrote treaties from year-to-year

    With no Indian rights, there were many bloody fights

In Canada
    For treaties the two parties did negotiate
    The white government did not commonly violate
    For changes there was two-party re-negotiation
    For what they gave up, Indians received compensation

    Everybody came out ahead, with very little bloodshed

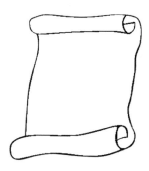

INDIAN KILLERS

White people killed many Indians.
Indians killed more Indians
　　　than the white people did.
Disease killed more Indians
　　　than the Indians did,
　　　　some of the diseases
　　　　from white people.
Indians killed many white people.

All of this killing has stopped.
It is now part of history.
What have we learned from it?

BUFFALO

To the Indians of the Great Plains
Buffalo were food, clothing, and shelter
In one of the great white blood stains
White men killed them all, helter-skelter

Buffalo have been called Indian cattle
They even used the buffalo chips for fires
Why would they give them up without a battle?
Just to satisfy the white man's desires?

Some whites wanted no buffalo preservation
Including the U.S. Secretary of the Interior
So Indians would return to the reservation
So, these white men's motives were ulterior

Buffalo numbered over sixty million at the peak
But after all the crowding out and flying lead
After all the fun and money white men seek
By 1900 there were only a thousand living head

END OF THE TRAIL

After their final defeat by white men
The Kiowa chiefs came to tragic end
White Bear jumped from the second story
Sitting Bear attacked his guards, went out in glory

Lone Wolf and Sky Walker to Florida in exile
Where life for Kiowas was a daily trial
Kicking Bird poisoned for singling them out
Though he saved many others from that route

Geronimo was the last Apache chief to be free
Defeated by five thousand mounted cavalry
Which was hardly a cause to celebrate
For Geronimo's band numbered only thirty-eight

Quanah Parker was half-Indian, half-white
As Comanche chief he was leader of their fight
After the Adobe Walls and Palo Duro losses
He worked among the whites for Comanche causes

No threat to whites, Chief Joseph and the Nez Perces
Until the army came to take their valley away
From tribe and homeland the Chief was kept apart
The doctor said that he died of a broken heart

Chief Sitting Bull of the Sioux, his fighting done
Was still feared by the white men who won
Taken from his cabin, he drew his last breath
When agents of the white man shot him to death

As the Indian way of life came to an end
Being chief was not what it had been
As white men came to hold full sway
All power of the Indian chiefs was taken away

The Soldiers

BARBARIANS OF THE BORDER

Confederate guerilla bands arose from the mud
To bathe the Kansas-Missouri border in blood
The raiders of William Clarke Quantrill
And of Anderson, known as Bloody Bill

Frank James rode with both these men
With Anderson, brother Jesse joined in the sin
They both learned their killing craft
They shot and burned and then laughed

The Union man brought to the scene
General Thomas Ewing was not very keen
Though his saber he might rattle
He could not defeat the rebels in battle

What a brave man was he
Targeting the civilians of Missouri
Residents of four counties on the border
To women and children, he gave no quarter

He ordered them out within fifteen days
Homes, farms, livestock; no buts or nays
He wanted to take away the rebels' support
With this evil tactic of last resort

Among his troops, war crimes were committed
Prosecution apparently was not permitted
This was not the Union's finest hour
Looting, burning, murdering for false power

The Confederate raiders continued unabated
Their support deepened, not what was anticipated
Wider across the state of Missouri it went
Achieving the opposite of Ewing's intent

And after the Civil War had ended
Gaining popular support, which was not intended
For the James and Younger gangs it appears
Helping the James boys roam for fifteen years

Ewing's conduct was beneath contempt
From punishment he was not totally exempt
His infamous Order Number Eleven
Did not give him a ticket to heaven

The Devil, Ewing, Anderson, and Quantrill
Sitting around a lava rock smoldering still
Playing a hot game of poker in hell
The Devil says, "All of you did well."

LITTLE BIGHORN

White man or red man to be the master
It surely was a recipe for disaster
They were both fully loaded for battle
Nobody was out on the range countin' cattle

Sitting Bull had his dream and put out the call
At the summer council, he wanted them all
The six clans of the Western Sioux
The Northern Cheyenne and Arapaho, too

General Custer, the white man in charge
Had an ego that was much too large
He had bragged that with him at the reins
His cavalry could beat all the Indians on the plains

But, not in ascendancy was Custer's star
He had been a temporary general in the Civil War
Actually, a light colonel in this battle so bad
Plus, he had made President Grant so mad

Custer was known as bold, but overstepped his orders
He was not known as loyal to his headquarters
For him, this was a time of desperation and abomination
Win a big battle, redeem the Presidential nomination

Sitting Bull had brought the Sioux to Crow land
Not to Dakota as tradition would demand
Custer, identified with the Michigan town of Monroe
Now his destiny to be decided in the land of the Crow

Among his scouts were Arikara, a.k.a. Ree
Who lived in earthen homes on the Missouri
A deaf ear to all his scouts: Ree, Crow, and white
To help himself, he saw one last chance to get it right

The cavalry was outnumbered ten to one
And the Sioux had a much better gun
Custer's rifles were single-shot and overheated
The Sioux had a better rifle that repeated

Custer split his small force into three
Ensuring the loss of the Seventh Cavalry
Custer, Reno, and Benteen in command
Custer rode off to make his last stand

Benteen was sent off on a wild goose chase
Custer and Reno wound up in the wrong place
Separately, and unknown to each of these two
They both charged right into the mass of the Sioux

Custer and his two hundred troops were all slain
Reno's men hit by bullets and arrows, falling like rain
Benteen arrived to help keep most of Reno's men alive
The thousands of Sioux withdrew, reinforcements arrived

Custer lost the battle and Presidential nomination
He lost his life and his remaining reputation
The Sioux won the battle, survived the strife
But still, all the Indians lost their way of life

THE BUFFALO SOLDIERS

During the Indian Wars on the Plains
    One of the little known facts
Was the four regiments of soldiers
    Who were Blacks

The Indians thought that their hair
    Resembled the buffalo's shaggy coat
So they called them, quote
    The Buffalo Soldiers, unquote

The Indians respected them
    And were always on their guard
For The Buffalo soldiers
    Fought frequently and hard

They did better soldiering than whites
    A fact that is undeniable
They had a lower desertion rate
    More stamina, more reliable

But battle reports for white troops
    Extolled virtues, page after page
Whereas, The Buffalo Soldiers
    reported as merely "engaged"

MARCUS PEEPUS

Marcus Reno was his real name
At Little Bighorn he gained his fame
For Custer's loss he was not to blame
But a court of inquiry was needed all the same

Reno's troop almost suffered Custer's fate
For on that tragic summer date
Many cavalrymen walked through the pearly gate
But Benteen's troop arrived before it was too late

Reno was found innocent of any wrong
His record in the Civil War had been strong
And his career as a major continued along
Though, perhaps his heart not filled with song

Then after the passage of another year
He was to be thrown out on his ear
For drawing a commander's wife too near
But President Hayes said that was too severe

He received a two year suspension of rank instead
Though by now things must be spinning in his head
All the things that people had said
And all the men he had seen dead

Six months back to rank, on a dark Dakota night
The commander's daughter sitting by a parlor light
Reno staring at her through the window a sudden sight
It gave the young lady Ella quite a fright

Out of love Marcus said he did peep
But a court-martial he did reap
And this time he was in trouble too deep
They threw him out in a troubled heap

FETTERMAN'S LAST STAND

William Fetterman and George Custer
Brimming with confidence and bluster
Were like two peas in a pod
They both answered only to God

Successful warriors in the Civil War
Temporary ranks lost to force-reduction
Lieutenant Colonel Fetterman to Captain
Brigadier General Custer to Lieutenant Colonel

Two inflated egos with braggadocio
Fetterman said that, with eighty men
He could split the Sioux Nation into two
Custer said, with his cavalry, rule the Plains

Both braggarts had no respect for their foe
Nor did they respect their superiors
Both disobeyed direct, specific orders
And advanced their troops beyond limits

Ironically, Fetterman did command eighty men
When he was ambushed in Wyoming
Along the Bozeman Trail leading to Montana
Custer and his men died north in Montana

Fetterman's force was divided into two
Custer divided his force into three
Fetterman's eighty ambushed by two thousand Sioux
Custer's two hundred attacked fifteen thousand Sioux

Just after their deaths in battle
Both were acclaimed as heroes
But when the truth came to light
Both were then known as fools

Fetterman had eighty men at his side
All eighty men fought and died
In this battle ten years, B.C.
Ten years Before Custer, you see

No history book was read from the shelf
So history repeated itself

DEVIL IN A BLUE COAT

As the Holy Bible duly advises
The devil wears many disguises
John Chivington wore one most sinister
After he wore the cloth of Methodist minister

He ran a church in Denver
Organized a Sunday school
Preached throughout the mining towns
Became an elder of Rocky Mountain Methodists

When offered a commission as chaplain
In Colorado's First Regiment of troops
He refused, demanded a commission to fight
And he did fight for the Union in the Civil War

Then he became leader of the regiment
"I believe I could run an empire," he said
But all summer long his troops chased Indians
His ambitions and ego were frustrated

Chivington said many fiendish things
Such as, "I want to be wading in gore."
I want to kill and scalp all,
big and little. Nits make lice."

"Damn any man who sympathizes with Indians!
I have come to kill all Indians,
and I believe it is right to use
any means under God's heaven!"

He decided to attack the village on Sand Creek
Home to Chief Black Kettle of the Cheyenne
The Indians were located here in compliance
With specific state and federal orders

Black Kettle had always argued for peace
Reasoning there were too many whites to fight
He had met with President Lincoln in Washington
The tribes were responding to his influence

Chivington led seven hundred troops
Against the village of five hundred Indians
Two-thirds of them women and children
Most warriors were hunting far away

When the army approached the village
Black Kettle raised the American flag
President Lincoln had given him
And then a white flag of surrender

The soldiers responded with rifle, pistol and cannon
Unarmed women and children were gunned down
Babies brains were bashed out against trees
Dead bodies were scalped and cut open

At first, the soldiers were heroes to the white race
But as the truth came out, it became a disgrace
And the minister turned colonel revealed
As the devil in a blue coat concealed

ROLL CALL

The Quest

Overall, the Army did its assigned job in the Old West.
>Kill and restrict the Indians.
>Provide some protection to white settlers.

The nobility of the purpose was more imagined than real.
>Kill and displace another race: destroy their culture.
>Manifest Destiny, the alleged will of God,
>that white people occupy America
>from ocean to ocean.

The Common Soldier

The life of the common soldier summed up in forty words:

>hard, tiring, uncomfortable, sore
>thirsty, hungry, sleepy
>painful, wounded, diseased
>hot, dirty, dry, dusty, windy
>stormy, rainy, wet, muddy, damp
>cold, snowy, icy, frost-bit
>hilly, rocky, slippery
>buggy, snakey, ratty
>dangerous, scary, risky
>thankless, abused, controlled
>lonely, boring, sexless, broke

The number of deserters was high (wonder why?)

Overall, the sergeants, corporals, and privates were tough, and did their jobs well enough.

ROLL CALL (Continued)

The Officers

As a group, the officers can be described in ten words:

>brave, physically-tough, hard-driving,
>ambitious, persistent, self-serving, egotistical,
>unknowledgeable, cruel, racist

Three factors worked against the officers:

>Their experience in the Civil War
>had limited value in the Indian Wars,
>because the geography was different,
>and the enemy fought differently.

>Many were triple demoted after the Civil War,
>due to downsizing, which made them
>overly-ambitious and jealous of one another.

>Men and supplies were limited,
>and hard to move around.

Generals Sherman and Sheridan, the top commanders,
>had many pluses and minuses.

Others were self-serving and foolish,
>such as Custer and Fetterman.

Colonel Carrington was inept.
>Colonel Chivington was a fiend.

Among the top officers in the Old West,
>It's hard to find a hero.

General George Crook may have been the best.

ROLL CALL (Continued)

Best in the West

William Tecumseh Sherman, the top commander
in the West, said of George Crook:
> "The greatest Indian fighter
> and manager the U.S. Army ever had."

Crook's men respected and liked him.
They composed and sang ballads about him.
> In contrast, Custer's top Captain,
> Frederick Benteen, said of Custer,
>> "I'm only too proud to say I despised him."

Apaches regarded Crook as their most dangerous foe,
> but admired him because
> he could be trusted to keep his word,
> and because he fought man-to-man, Apache style.

He fought the Apaches hard, and defeated them,
> but when the war in the southwest was over,
> he helped the Apaches start new ways of life.

He considered them human beings,
> rather than mindless savages.

The Women

THE OUTLAW GIRLS
--And Wild Women of the West

They were equal opportunity employers
    Butch Cassidy, Cole Younger, and Bill Doolin
    They had women in their gangs, no foolin'

Laura Bullion had no heart of gold
    You wouldn't want to invite her to lunch
    She was a member of Butch's Wild Bunch

Belle Starr had a fling with Cole Younger
    She must have been pretty mean
    For she was known as the bandit queen

Pearl Hart from down Arizona way
    Wanted to be among the very tops
    At causing unscheduled stagecoach stops

Poker Alice, chomping on her cigar
    Really lived up to her quaint name
    For gambling was her risky game

Calamity Jane's first name was Martha
    This notorious wild woman of the West
    Sure did like to stir up a hornet's nest

Cattle Annie and sidekick Little Britches
    Were lucky that they didn't hang
    As gun-totin' members of Bill Doolin's gang

The wild men you'd heard about before
    Doc Holliday, Billy the Kid, and Jesse James
    Now you know the wild women's names

A WESTERN WOMAN'S WORKDAY

Up before daybreak
Fire up the stove
And bake a cake

Pour water in the pot
Grind the coffee beans
Charley likes it hot

Feed all the little dickens
Wash the dishes
Then feed the chickens

Keep your gun nearby
Watch and listen for
An Indian war cry

Slop the sows
Grab the pail
Milk the cows

Gather the eggs
Mend Charley's pants
And shorten the legs

Milk from the udder
Churn away until
It turns to butter

Check the traps for mice
During the night
Something squeaked twice

From the old stump
Take the bucket
Fill it at the pump

While you heat water
Go fork the cows
Some hay and fodder

Scrub the dirty clothes
Sing while you work
To chase the lonely woes

Chop weeds in the garden
Hoe up the dirt
So it won't harden

Sling the horse's saddle
Ride the range
Check the cattle

With gun and fish hook
Shoot a prairie chicken
Catch trout in the brook

Cook dinner before it's late
"Wash up, children.
Come load your plate."

Clear the table off
Mix an elixir
For Suzy's cough

Tuck the children away
Quilt a square
Ask Charley about his day

Another child on Earth
Because at midnight
You give him birth

Sleep now, maybe
Up early tomorrow
Bathe the baby

First thing out of bed
Make some candles
Bake some bread

MRS. CUSTER'S LAST STAND

When Custer and his men died at Little Bighorn
Many army wives were left to mourn

At Fort Abraham Lincoln, news of the fatalities
Turned the women's worst fears into realities

When Captain McCaskey knocked on her back door
Elizabeth Custer did not collapse upon the floor

She threw a wrap over her dressing gown
And helped the other wives not fall down

She went with the captain to spread the news
To twenty-five women who husbands did lose

She consoled each and every one at the fort
Gave them her shoulder and support

Later she could shed her own tears
Later she could face her own fears

But she rose to what the occasion did demand
As the commander's wife, she made her last stand

A WOMAN'S PLACE

Nineteenth century men and women agreed
A woman's place is in the home they decreed
But for a certain kind of woman there might be
In that Old West, a window of opportunity
If she raised the roof, kicked in the door
And stomped her feet upon the floor

Arizona Mary was a bullwhacker
And nobody dared to attack her
Wearing her long dress and sun bonnet
Freight wagon with eight yoke of oxen on it
With the loud crack of her bullwhip
And curses rolling off her full lip

Black Mary was a former slave
Who became one of the bravest of the brave
Six feet tall and two hundred pounds
Hard fists, a rifle, a shooter with six rounds
Fat cigar in her mouth, and a jug of whiskey
She demanded and got R-E-S-P-E-C-T

Nellie Cashman traveled the gold fields back and forth
From Tombstone in the south to Klondike in the north
A pretty, petite woman who stood only five feet
As restaurateur, hotelier, grocer she did meet
And feed and care for the miners, under sun and moon
They all stood up whenever she walked into a saloon

Elsa Jane Forest dressed up as a fake man
Worked the riverboats, and railroaded as a brakeman
Continued to work in her male masquerade
In the mule, freighting, ranching, and fur trade
Becoming addicted to her male entity
Because she could go anywhere and feel free

Lucille Mulhall won the roping and riding contest
At steer wrestling, bronc busting, and roping was best
In her long dress, gloves, and fashionable hat
She beat all the men, and that was that
In the original wild west show swirl
She was known as "The Original Cowgirl"

Martha Maxwell was first at many things
As she studied animals; paws, hoofs and wings
The only woman naturalist of her time
Rocky Mountain hunter, taxidermist, artist sublime
At the U.S. Centennial it was no real quirk
Her lifelike display was entitled "Woman's Work"

These western women of free spirit and strong will
They climbed the slope, looked over the hill
They threw off the shackles of the East
Looked life in the eye, and slew the beast
They said, in that Old West window of opportunity
A woman's place was where a woman wanted to be

A WOMAN'S TOUCH

Some say the wild west was won
By the lead and powder of a gun
But it was tamed just as much
By the power of a woman's touch

The first white settlers were all men
Prostitution was the first job open then
For these young women's tender touch
The question simply was, "How much?"

Later came single women looking for marriage
And married women by covered wagon carriage
With such women on the pioneer scene
Men improved their personal hygiene

To protect the objects of their romances
With the Indians, men took fewer chances
With women in their wagon train, it seems
Men took better care of their wagon teams

When women took over the cooking pot
The number of sick men went down a lot
All the food had a much better taste
And much less food went to waste

Women wanted schools for their offspring
And churches in which to pray and sing
They started libraries with books to read
And charities to help those in need

Western men often drank beyond moderation
So along came bible-waving Carry Nation
With her trusty hatchet, she busted up saloons
Fancy mirrors, ornate bars, shiny spittoons

Women brought the Old West the graces of life
Better social order and much less strife
Civilized communities, amenities and such
All the wonders of a woman's touch

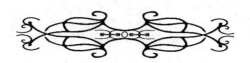

The Prostitutes

HATS OFF TO THE LADIES

In the old brothel tent
Almost anything went
They had just one rule
Broken only by a fool

To be serviced by prostitutes
You could keep on your boots
But if you wanted some of that
You had to take off your hat

Lined up, ready with the money
Waitin' for a taste of the honey
Standin' there, in a motley band
They came with hat in hand

ALL ABOARD!

This is the steam generation
    All aboard!
This train is leaving the station

Towns along the railroad tracks
    Clickety-clack!
Working girls on their backs

Now getting dark in the town
    Whoosh!
Time to shut the engine down

Trainmen, before you go tonight
    Scritch! Scritch!
Light your red lantern's light

If you go to see yourself a whore
    Knock! Knock!
Hang your lantern by the door

The red light district
    Choo! Choo!
Don't it look artistic?

All aboard!

PILLOW NAMES

An actress performs upon the stage
And has a stage name

A writer writes upon the page
And has a pen name

A prostitute performs upon the bed
And has a pillow name

Some had names you might hear any day
Jennie Rogers, Mary Smith, and Anna Gray

Some had names to suit their professional state
Dirty Alice, Blonde Marie, and Rowdy Kate

Some had names that bring worry of pain
Squirrel Tooth Alice, Mustang Mae, Calamity Jane

Adobe Moll was formerly Mary Callaghan
Maggie Hall became Molly b'Dam

Mary Ann Boyer became Madame Damnable
Eleanora Dumont became Madame Moustache

Mary Welch became Chicago Joe on her pillow
Lottie Ables Pickett became Sorrel Mike, you know

Josephine Marcus married Wyatt Earp, they say
Big Nose Kate was companion to Doc Holliday

Now, the "good time" girls will keep their fames
Because now we know their pillow names

MADAMS GALORE

In the old western days of yore
There were madams galore

A hundred men per woman, what solution?
In the old west, it was prostitution

To run a parlor, brothel, or crib
You needed a madam from Adam's rib

Such as Ella Hill in Amarillo
And Ah Toy in San Francisco

From Molly b'Dam in Murray, Idaho
To Molly Silks in Denver, Colorado

Virginia Slade in Virginia City, Nevada
And Chicago Joe in Helena, Montana

From Laura Evans in Salida
To Madame Damnable in Seattle

Most madams remembered their roots
And took good care of their prostitutes

Some were wonderful community patrons
Though scorned by the respectable matrons

DAYDREAMS AND NIGHTMARES
--Song of the Soiled Doves

I can be a painted lady of the parlour house
I can stroll the promenade with my parasol
I can sing and dance to the tune of the piano man
I can smoke and charm and drug and drink
I can be the belle of the ball, then go down the hall
And march to the tune of the man with money

Money, adventure and freedom we seek
Wearing the latest fashions, eating the good food
Accepting the will of all sorts of men
But given little or none of the money earned
Given no rights or respect by the townspeople
Welcome to the world of the working girls

Quickly aging and beauty fading
Dropping from parlour house to brothel to "hog farm"
Men in muddy boots sharing your bed and body
Confined to your room all day, with sex all night
Daydreams all turned to nightmares
We die young of disease, drugs, suicide, or murder

In San Francisco, men went wild for Chinese girls
"Two bitee lookee, flo bitee feelee, six bitee doee"
The nightly cry from the cribs of the sing-song girls
Girls sold by their parents in China
Enslaved, brought to America, abused in every way
Used up at twenty, murder or suicide their destiny

The Miners

GOLD FEVER

I got the gold fever
I got a wife, too
But I gotta leave'er

Just layin' on the ground
They're pickin' up big chunks
Just waitin' there to be found

By a wagon or a boat
Men are goin' to California
Anything that'll roll or float

Around the Cape of Good Hope
Through the jungles of Panama
Across plains and mountain slope

Depending on the chosen route
Two thousand, ten thousand miles
Goin' to dig that gold out !

Farmers leavin' crops in the field
Teachers leavin' kids in the dark
How much will that ore yield?

When they heard the good news
Golden light shining in their eyes
Pastors left their flocks in the pews

When you get that gleam in your eyes
And become a true believer
Then you say your good-byes

Passengers and crew
After a nine month journey
What did they do?

They all left the next day
Ships swinging at anchor
In San Francisco Bay

Planks rotting away
Cargo still on board
Nobody on the quay

Nobody to retrieve'er
All gone to the gold fields
They all got the gold fever

FLASH IN THE PAN
--With Riffles and Riddles

I'm swishin' the water fast as I can
I'm watchin' for a flash in the pan

Dumpin' gravel in the cradle hopper
A bucket a water atop a her
Rockin' like a baby in the cradle would
Hopin' to catch gold on the strips a wood

And the dirt and the water goes in here
And nothin' comes out there
And the dirt and the water goes in here
And the gold comes out there

We got a Long Tom with holes in the riddle
Washin' dirt and water down the middle
Strained into the open box through the riddle
In the bottom to catch the gold, strips of riffle

And the dirt and the water goes in here
And nothin' comes out there
And the dirt and the water goes in here
And the gold comes out there

We're shovelin' dirt into the sluice
Where the water pours like juice
A bunch of riffle boxes in the sluice
To trap the heavy, heavy gold like a noose

Pan, cradle, Long Tom, or sluice
We gotta wash that gold loose
Picks and shovels workin' hard as it takes
Lookin' for nuggets, dust, and flakes

I'm swishin' the water fast as I can
I'm watchin' for a flash in the pan

FAIRY STARS

Stars always have lighted the sky
Young girls always have floated by
Miners, miners growing more wise
Fairy stars dancing before their eyes

They had left wives and children behind
They had left all with whom they intertwined
To see a child, any child in the far West
Thrilled the heart beating under the vest

When Yankee Robinson put Little Sue on stage
The crowd of rough miners driven to rage
They clapped and yelled, threw hats into the air
Thrilled to see such a tender talent up there

And then one day right across the street
A young and talented girl came to compete
Little Lotta Crabtree was her name
She sang and danced her way to fame

Whether they found California gold or not
Miners' hides were tanned and softened a lot
While looking into the sky for Venus and Mars
They were touched by the little fairy stars

BABY DOE

For miners in the Old West
Boom and bust was the way of life
Baby Doe lived it as a miner's wife

Baby Doe was born Lizzie McCourt
Her lifestyle in Oshkosh quite nice
Until the town burned down twice

She married into a well-to-do family
Becoming Mrs. W.H. "Harvey" Doe
And together they moved to Colorado

Her thrill and adventure soon palled
Harvey failed with his father's prospect
And with every other mining aspect

She took long walks around Central City
Among miners her beauty gave her fame
So they gave her the "Baby" Doe name

Years later she met a man in Leadville
He was H.A.W. Tabor, the Silver King
Many millions his mines did bring

Tabor and Baby Doe became a pair
He lived an outgoing, fun-loving life
A different approach than his wife

Tabor and Baby Doe, both divorced
From spouses they seldom saw
Big plans for their wedding did draw

Tabor was a short-term Senator
Theirs a posh wedding in Washington, D.C.
President Chester A. Arthur an attendee

Tabor and Baby Doe lived a life of luxury
They were happy and true to each other
Twice, Baby Doe became a mother

Tabor contributed to churches and charities
Built opera houses in Denver and Leadville
Grubstaked anyone who couldn't pay the bill

The Tabors second marriage was a success
They were the wealth of Colorado society
But women lifted their noses in false piety

The Tabors continued their high living
Until the silver crash and the bank crash
Took away all their comfort and cash

For their very survival
Both Baby Doe and Tabor
Worked in the mines at manual labor

Tabor's dying words to his wife
"Never give up the Matchless Mine."
But it never produced another find

Thirty-six years a widow was she
Loyal to Tabor's dying request
To hang onto the Matchless

She clung to this last hope
Living in the tool cabin amongst the pine
By the hoist house and shaft of the mine

Baby Doe, feet wrapped in burlap
No money for clothes or shoes
Living and dying as you choose

Baby Doe, Baby Doe
Hungry and cold no more
Frozen to death on the cabin floor

For miners in the Old West
Boom and bust was the way of life
Baby Doe lived it as a miner's wife

BOOM AND BUST

Boom and bust was the miner's rule
Today we say, the finder was a fool
But our hindsight is twenty-twenty
The finders thought they had aplenty

One gold-finder right after another
Sold too low, too soon, like the other
From their discovery, they got little benefit
Too quick to get out, too soon to quit

John Sutter got very little for his mill
Others made millions before they got their fill
Henry Comstock got eleven thousand for his lode
For others, over a hundred million it flowed

Boom and bust was the miner's rule
Today we say, the finder was a fool
But our hindsight is twenty-twenty
The finders thought they had aplenty

WHITE GOLD

Humble mineral made not of silver or gold
But a profit to the miner of manyfold
From Nevada, and California's Death Valley
Miners and processors ran up a huge tally

From the hottest place with sun shining bright
Deposits on the ground, gleaming white
Scooping it up, and to nature giving thanks
Refined in dissolving, settling, crystalizing tanks

Hauled from the desert in custom-made wagons
Two hitched together, carrying over thirty tons
Pulled by a team of twenty, sturdy mules
With long whip and jerkline the driver rules

Not an ornament or gem that amuses
But a mineral of many and varied uses
From cleanser, medicine, and antiseptics
To enamel, playing cards, and cosmetics

Made of sodium, oxygen, boron, and water
Gathered from a desert that couldn't be hotter
Now that you know all of these facts
You know the old western story of borax

WESTERN BONANZA

By force and by negotiations
The western states were acquired
From Indian and foreign nations

Many in the Louisiana Purchase from France
California and Texas from Mexico
From Russia, the great Alaskan expanse

Nobody knew what treasures might abound
Until American settlers trickled in
And gold and silver were found

The first big thrill
Was the California gold
At Sutter's mill

The biggest treasure flowed
In Nevada gold and silver
From the Comstock lode

The gold that many did seek
Was found in Colorado
Along Cripple Creek

Jacksonville, Oregon produced gold so fine
And for silver in Idaho
It was the Bunker Hill Mine

The gunfight at O.K. Corral is well-known
Meanwhile, the mine outside town
Was producing silver at Tombstone

Among many a lucky strike
Gold in the Black Hills of Dakota
And the gold rush to the Klondike

Americans and immigrants had no peers
As placer and hard-rock miners
The Western Bonanza lasting over fifty years

The Gamblers

INDIAN GAMES

Long before the white man did arrive
Gambling among the Indians did thrive
Stakes could include a horse, gun, or knife
Food, clothes, or even a man's wife

Bets on sleight-of-hand games among Crow
Also, Kiowa, Cheyenne, Ute, and Arapaho
Dice were tossed with bets on the throw
Among Assiniboin, Dakota, and Papago

Wagers on foot races popular, we know
Among Zuni, Hopi, Pima, and Navajo
Horse races for Hidatsa and Minataree
Archery contests for the Mandan and Pawnee

Gambling sometimes part of ancient ceremonies
But not for Yakimas, Apaches, or Shoshonis
They played card games from the white man
Though Indians gambled since history began

GAMBLING FEVER

In the Old West gambling was feverishly intense
It hasn't been as dominant before or since
It's always a risky business say the oddsmakers
But the men who went west were risk-takers

Gambling was everywhere you looked
If there was a chance, bets were booked
Gambling seemed to be every place
Some of it out in the wide open space

> *Miners by a stream or breaking hard rock*
> *Dealing cards, sipping whiskey from a crock*
>
> *Cowboys out on the range or in the bunkhouse*
> *The boys that lose, they sure do grouse*
>
> *Indians in camp or out on the plains*
> *Taking their losses, counting their gains*
>
> *Railroad builders at the railhead*
> *Dealing a few hands, falling into bed*
>
> *Soldiers from the remote fort*
> *Keeping the light low, to stay off report*
>
> *Buffalo hunters sitting on a stack of hides*
> *Betting on whatever the dealer provides*
>
> *Lumberjacks out in cabin or forest glade*
> *On into the darkness they played*

When the men came to town with money
For gambling, whiskey, and local honey
They had worked up a big appetite
And whooped it up day and night

Joined at the tables by professional gamblers
Gunfighters, robbers, politicians, and ramblers
Most of them were just passing through
But a lot of townsfolk were there, too

Bankers, storekeepers, and preachers
Gambling with workers and criminal creatures
Some gamblers were also masters with a gun
Such as lawmen Wyatt Earp and Bat Masterson

In Kansas, at the end of the Texas cattle drive
Boomtowns where not everybody got out alive
Gambling, drinking, whoring, and gun play
In Abilene, Ellsworth, and Fort Dodge every day

The mining boomtowns had the same features
More saloons and casinos than schoolteachers
For gambling, Leadville, Deadwood, and Tombstone
With Denver and San Francisco held their own

Many a man, when he finally awoke
Found himself stone-cold broke
The hides or cattle he had turned into cash
His wages or gold gone in a flash

By professional gamblers, outplayed or cheated
To rotgut whiskey and ugly women, they were treated
But often the men left town happy as a king
Feeling that they had had one hell of a fling!

WHITE MAN GAMES

In the Old West some games that gamblers ran
Were played by Mexicans, Indians, and the white man
Though there was some gambling between the races
Most white men gambled in white man places

Some of the games we don't play much anymore
Such as Forty-five, Seven Up, and All Fours
Some of the old games are lost in the foggy mist
Such as Cassino, Chuck-a-Luck, and Whist

But some of the games westerners used to play
Such as euchre and poker, we still play today
Vingt-et-un, twenty-one, we call blackjack
Another French game, rouge-et-noir, red and black

Another way to stray from the straight and narrow
Was a game from France called faro
The thing that kept the player feeling vexed
He had to bet on which card would be dealt next

Keno seems a bit like Bingo, a row across won
Numbered wooden balls were dropped one-by-one
From a spinning container called the goose
For a lucky gambler, a golden egg might drop loose

Three card Monte was the old shell game
They used cards and gave it a new name
Sleight-of-hand was still the rule
The cards were moved too fast for the fool

Wagers were placed days and nights
On cock fights, dog fights, and fist fights
On steamboat races and stagecoach races
On horses being put through their paces

Bets were placed on the spinning of a wheel
Bets on lotteries and billiards also a big deal
Many a fortune rode on the roll of the dice
One time they even bet on the melting of ice!

PREACHER BROWN

In the old days of the Klondike gold rush
There was a man known as Preacher Brown
He found himself in the dead of Alaska's winter
Marooned by a blizzard in a small town

Whiskey and gambling occupied the miners
They treated the preacher like a damn joker
When he said they needed to fund a church
They challenged him to win the money at poker

They taunted him and asked if he knew how to play
Finally, he had enough of their being funny
He sat down and softly said, "Give me some chips."
Then he proceeded to win all their money

What none of the Alaskan scoffers knew
About Preacher Brown from down Nevada way
Was that he was a reformed professional cardsharp
Who backslid to win them a church that icy day

DIRTY DEALING

Professional gamblers liked to compete
And most of them loved to cheat
With nimble fingers they did sleight-of-hand
With a marked deck, they were in command

Some manufacturers marked decks, it was known
But the true professionals liked to mark their own
With subtle cuts along the edge
Their big bets they hedged

On the back of the cards, in the fancy design
They could hide their mark with scroll and line
A spot of water would remove the glaze
Leaving the suckers in a haze

Poking tiny holes in selected cards couldn't fail
Reading them with their fingers like Braille
Tinting the backs of the cards with dye
Varying the shades and the cards don't lie

Dealing seconds, the same card on top, succeeded
If they kept it there until it was needed
Dealing from the bottom of the deck worked, too
If you kept the good cards on top for you

A false shuffle or a phony cut they could dare
If they already knew which card was where
Ring in a cooler meant sneak in a stacked deck
Quicker than any eye could detect

A card up the sleeve or under the vest
An ace in the hole could beat all the rest
A shiner could show an opponent's hand
Reflected in a mirror as the cards were fanned

A gambler's tricks worked like magic
But if discovered, the results were tragic
In a brief moment of shock and dread
A gunshot could leave the gambler dead

Post Mortem

So if I had been in your shoes
I would rather deal square and lose
You never gave a sucker an even break
All you did was take and take

You knew if found to be dirty dealing
You could wind up staring at the ceiling
Now that you have had your thrill
You now will be buried in Boot Hill

CHINATOWN GAMES

San Francisco had a thousand places to put a bet down
Two hundred of them were in Chinatown
Around Portsmouth Square white bettors would meet
Chinese in Ross Alley, Dupont, and Sacramento Street

Dots on the dice and dots on the dominoes
Two games that all Chinatown knows
They play dominoes at such high speed
It would make a white man's nose bleed

"White Pigeon Ticket" was a funny name
For a popular Chinese lottery game
In China the game was against the law
So pigeons carried the ticket above the claw

In fan-tan the dealer covered several tokens with a cup
Fanned them out, and four at a time, raked them up
After bets were down on zero, one, two, or three
Which was how many remaining tokens there might be

In the Old West gamblers were everywhere
White men coming west from the East, and east of there
Native Americans and Mexicans played with great zest
As did Chinese coming east from the Far East to the West

... AND SO IT GOES

Gambling was thought acceptable year after year
Until towns matured and the evils became clear
Killings, economic disruptions, so many did lose
Gamblers cheating, all the floozies and booze

The railroad builders put so many tracks down
Cowboys could drive the cattle to a nearby town
Buffalo hunters ran out of buffalo to kill
Miners ran out of rich ore, from stream or hill

Lumberjacks cut down most of the forestation
The soldiers killed or put Indians on the reservation
As the Old West settled down and caught its breath
The old gambling fever died a natural death

The Spanish

EL DRAGÓN
--An Ode to Drake

The sailor son of a farmer man was he
Sailing the seven seas was his specialty

The second circumnavigation of the globe he did make
Of defeating the Spanish Armada he did partake

The Union Jack or the Jolly Roger run up and down
His ships still sailed for the English crown

The Spaniards called him the dragon, El Dragón
Over the Spanish American seas he did roam

Tons of the gold that the Spanish stole
Wound up deep down in his ship's hold

Queen Elizabeth said the Spanish King wanted his head
With a gold sword, she knighted him Sir Francis instead

LA CORONA Y LA CRUZ
--For Crown and Cross

To Texas, New Mexico, Arizona, California
To states we now call by name
North from Mexico, the Spaniards came

For crown and cross, soldiers and priests together
The priests sought to save the Indian's soul
The soldiers sought to steal the Indian's gold

In the name of Jesus Christ and the King of Spain
They had already brought death and degradations
To the very advanced Inca and Aztec civilizations

Unlike the already exploited Incas and Aztecs
No great wealth had the Indians of the southwest
So the Spaniards were delusional in their quest

To the American Indians they brought diseases
Coronado and others burned Indians at the stake
Their food and homes they did heartlessly take

Hundreds of souls were saved
Hundreds of thousands of lives were lost
Soldiers and priests together, for crown and cross

CALIFORNIOS
--On a Mythical Island

From San Diego to San Francisco
Twenty-one missions were built
Each one a day's ride to the next
All within the Spanish Catholic context

The priests worked hard to save the Indians' souls
Then the Indians worked hard on more earthly goals
They tended the crops and livestock of the mission
They were not allowed to leave without permission

When Mexico gained independence from Spain
Power shifted from religious to political domain
The mission lands were given to the rancheros
Whose cattle were tended by the vaqueros

Cattle were all over the California landscape
Fruits, vegetables, and the mighty grape
Some sheep here and there they did allow
Pigs were raised only for soap tallow

Weddings and fiestas with guitars and violins
Music taught by the priests to the Indians
Wild horses and races and riding skills
 Bullfights and cockfights, bets on the kills

The Spanish and Mexican governments decreed
No visitors allowed, a rule Californios paid no heed
French, English, and Russians they hosted
Tops in hospitality they could have boasted

Californios were an independent breed
The bountiful land and each other their only need
The name California, from a mythical island was taken
Far from the seats of power, Spain and Mexico forsaken

Some favored joining with Britain or France for defense
But Californios liked America's spirit of independence
After the logic of Mariano Vallejo won the debate
California became a magical American state

FELIZ NAVIDAD !
--The Lone Star is Born

In 1821 Texas was a province of Mexico
Then in a show of some bravado
Stephen Austin settled on the Colorado

At the Alamo, with Colonel Travis in command
Jim Bowie, Davy Crockett, and 180 made their stand
They all fought to the death of the last man

In 1836 it was "Remember the Alamo"
Santa Anna leading the troops of Mexico
Sam Houston beat him at the battle of San Jacinto

Texas was the Lone Star Republic for ten years
Having overcome their Comanche and Mexican fears
Though not yet giving their loudest cheers

Then in 1846 Texas became the Lone Star state
Into the Union at number twenty-eight
Province to republic to state was the Texan fate

Feliz Navidad !

EL GENERAL AMERICANO
--Old Rough and Ready

Why he was the way he was
Nobody knows
But Old Rough and Ready
Mended his own clothes

Others wore ostrich plumes on their heads
Measuring twenty inches or more
But Old Rough and Ready
Was bare-bones to the core

They said the odds were against him
When he sent his men into battle
But Old Rough and Ready
Sat calmly in his saddle

Both sides brought cannon to the front
Canister and grape shots into the fray
But Old Rough and Ready
Said bayonets would carry the day

They said disarm all the Mexicans
When their colors were struck
But Old Rough and Ready
Sent them home, down on their luck

Some hoped he then would go away
To wherever old soldiers went
But Old Rough and Ready
Then was elected President

SOLDADOS HERMANOS
--Brothers in Arms

They fought for the Manifest Destiny of the U.S. A.
They invaded Mexico to take land away

Santa Anna, President and General, on the Mexican side
Fought with greater numbers for Mexico's pride

Victor at the Alamo, loser at San Jacinto
In the Mexican War, he lost all his mojo

Troops from Texas and the Missouri Volunteers
From Tennessee and New York pinned back his ears

From Illinois, New Hampshire, and Arkansas
They fought the Mexicans tooth and claw

At Buena Vista, forming the winning vee
Indiana's third and the Rifles of Mississippi

Years before the Civil War had its start
Many young officers learned their art

Jefferson Davis and George McClellan fought hard
 Side-by-side with Meade and Beauregard

As brothers in arms they fought to victory
Ulysses S. Grant and Robert E. Lee

The River Boaters

ODE TO MUD
--The Mighty Missouri River

When westward expansion was our goal
Wagon trains and railroad trains played a role
The Missouri River, too, had a major part
From St. Louis, pioneers made their start

Longest river on the North American continent
From St. Louis to the Rockies they went
Three thousand winding miles upstream
Looking to fulfill their American dream

Riding on the muddy waters of the Missouri River
Many tributaries, their waters they do give'er
The Osage, Platte, Nebraska, and Cheyenne
The Poplar, Milk, Musselshell, and Grand

Also, the Gallatin, Yellowstone, and Chariton
Two tributaries pay tribute to Jefferson and Madison
Some tributaries have tributaries, like Yellowstone
As Powder, Tongue, and Big Horn they are known

Some tributaries of tributaries have tributaries, too
The Big Horn had the Little Bighorn, it's true
A twelve thousand mile network, all told
Waterways bearing mud, furs, and gold

They called it the Big Muddy, you know
A land of mountains, with ice and snow
A land of prairie dust and grassy plains
A river of mud and water and falling rains

UP THE WILD MISSOURI

Mississippi ice in the Missouri's craw
We're done waitin' for the spring thaw
Fire up the boiler, build up some steam
It's time we head up the damn stream

One big paddlewheel, spinnin' at the stern
Better than one each side is what we learn
Time to load up passengers and supplies
This time, I hope the hell nobody dies

On-load, off-load, onward she goes
When she stops along the way, whistle blows
Burnin' wood by the log and the cord
Swingin' into shore to take more aboard

Year by year, day by day, the channel sways
Laws of nature and the current it obeys
Sandbars come and sandbars go
Steamin' around or aground, up to the flow

Some places where the river narrows
Indians along the banks are shootin' arrows
Sometimes talkin' or tradin' will succeed
Sometimes firin' every gun does the deed

Speed is often the answer to our prayers
More wood in the firebox, as cinder flares
Runnin' from Indians or powerin' over sand
Speed gives us a real helpin' hand

Most paddle-wheelers don't last very long
The boilers blow up with steam too strong
They run into sunken trees or run aground
Or catch fire with a loud, cracklin' sound

Men workin' and fightin' and dyin'
Sparks, arrows, bullets, and flags flyin'
Against all odds, the Captain and the crew
Most of the time, we make it through!

FIRE AND ICE

St. Louis had steamboat disasters twice
Once by fire, and once by ice

On a night in May, eighteen forty-nine
Without a warning, without a sign
Fire broke out on the White Cloud
One of the steamboats in the port crowd

Quickly, the fire spread from vessel-to-vessel
So closely did all of the steamboats nestle
The flames jumped to buildings along the shore
Fifteen city blocks, twenty-three boats lost in the roar

Seven years later came hills and ridges of ice
Fifty barges and canal boats paid the price
Twenty blocks of steamboats ground to sticks
The Great Ice Gorge of eighteen and fifty-six

St. Louis had steamboat disasters twice
Once by fire, and once by ice

BAD DAY ON GOOD FRIDAY

The year was eighteen hundred and fifty-two
April ninth, Good Friday, a day to rue
At Lexington, Missouri was the spring flood
Now we know, it was out for blood

The Saluda was a tired, creaky, old boat
Once sunk by a snag, again it was afloat
For two days the river was the Captain's deterrent
He tried over and over to overcome the current

Goaded by passengers and onlookers ashore
The Captain was determined to try once more
He ordered the fireboxes filled with wood
He ordered the safety valve locked down good

In revolutions, the paddlewheels made only two
Before the double boilers blew!
Captain Belt and the ship's bell flew to a cliff-top
Then rolled clanging down to a final stop

The six hundred pound safe and its guard
Landed ashore about two hundred yard
People, cargo, and ship parts high in the air
Pieces of the boilers landing everywhere

The passengers, Mormons from England and Wales
Their goal was Salt Lake City via the Mormon Trails
One old steamboat all blown to hell
Two hundred Mormons blown to heaven, as well

A HUNDRED YEARS ON THE RIVER

The Missouri River was America's heartbeat
A key to our whole westward expansion feat
A time of great boldness amid awesome fears
The Nineteenth Century embraced its hundred years

It began with the journey of Lewis and Clark
And the fur trade that their reports did spark
Trappers upstream to their Rocky Mountain domains
Their furs downstream to St. Louis for dollar gains

Settlers with families and all their gear
Going west with everything they held dear
Miners to Montana and Idaho for unknown yields
Seeking their fortunes in the western goldfields

Steamboats served the army as troop transports
To Benton and Lincoln and all the other forts
As bearers of ammunition, food and supplies
As hospitals, gunboats, and added pairs of eyes

Indian canoes and bullboats with shallow draw
Then flatboats, keelboats, and the Mackinaw
Finally, side wheel and stern wheel steamboats
A hundred years of brave riders on whatever floats

It ended when the railroad arrived far and wide
Faster and more frequent schedules it did provide
The Iron Horse was truly feeling its oats
As it replaced the hundreds of wooden steamboats

The Nineteenth Century embraced its hundred years
A time of great boldness amid awesome fears
A key to our whole westward expansion feat
The Missouri River was America's heartbeat

The Freight Haulers

PONY EXPRESS

From St. Joe to Sacramento
    From Sacramento to St. Joe
Two thousand miles each way
    Ten days for riders in the relay

They advertised for daring young men
    Not for a coward or a has-been
They wanted courage not to be deterred
    They said orphans were preferred

Nineteen was the average rider's age
    We all competed with the slower stage
At fifteen, Buffalo Bill Cody was among us
    At thirteen, David Jay was the youngest

We all had our own riding styles
    Each day we rode seventy-five miles
Five times our horses we did change
    In two minutes we were back on the range

We rode through rain, sleet, and hail
    Arrows and bullets flying on our trail
We rode through the heat and the cold
    We didn't worry about living to be old

None of that stuff could beat us
    But the telegraph did defeat us
Though our ponies weren't quick to tire
    They couldn't keep up with the singing wire

BULLWHACKERS AND MULE SKINNERS

In springtime, wagons lined the Missouri River banks
From Independence to Council Bluffs in long ranks
Loading freight from the steamboat decks
Then wagon trains off on their westward treks

The drivers or teamsters were called
By the names of their animals who hauled
If oxen, they were bullwhackers
If mules, they were mule skinners

These names the teamsters took from their team
Really aren't quite what they seem
Bullwhackers didn't whack the bulls
Mule skinners didn't skin the mules

To whack a bull with a whip
Would take a big chunk with the tip
Leading to disease and demise of the bull
And everybody knows a dead bull can't pull

So they cracked the whip overhead
Just to keep the bulls on an even tread
But they didn't hit the bulls' backs
So bullwhackers were actually bullcrackers

Mule skinners followed the same whip rule
They didn't even like to skin a dead mule
Only if desperate were they mule snackers
So mule skinners were actually mule crackers

Actually, the bulls weren't bulls; they were steers
The mules <u>were</u> mules, but who cares !

STAGECOACH
--A Ride on the Wild Side

For six hundred bucks you could ride
From the Missouri to the Pacific tide
Two thousand miles, seventeen days away
Fifty horses and three drivers a day

Nine passengers inside, on top up to a dozen
Plus the driver and his shotgun rider cousin
You were bound to be cramped for space
Rocky roads bouncing you all over the place

Every single night was a sleepless night
Either lying on a dirt floor or sitting upright
The only beds in the stations not for you
They were only for the drivers and crew

Choking down dust and bad food
All the discomforts of a western dude
All this you would experience without fail
More, if you weren't lucky on the trail

A blizzard in spring as harsh as winter's
A wind gust smashing the stage to splinters
Coach breakdowns in the middle of the plains
Attacks by bandits looking for ill-gotten gains

Runaway team racing here and there
Indian arrows flying through the air
Hard rains, swollen rivers, and flash floods
Passenger illnesses, and impassable muds

On the good side, the adventure of a lifetime
Wild animals, and scenic beauty sublime
Crossing the western wilderness in its glory
Each passenger with a fascinating life story

Usually, getting there alive
Everybody happy as hell to arrive
Tales to tell, with adventurer's pride
Of the ride they had on the wild side

CHARLIE'S SURPRISE

Charlie Parkhurst drove a California stage
For thirty years, through the pine and sage
Reins in the left hand, whip in the right
In the glare of the sun, in the dark of night

He had the powers of a captain at sea
Everything about the stage, his responsibility
He had fought off the Indian attacks
Handled the hazards of the road tracks

Charlie was known to hitch up his pants
And have a go at a game of chance
He would knock back a drink or two
Bite off a chaw and have himself a chew

When older, he kept on handling the reins
Though wracked with rheumatism pains
He was still tough and acting spry
Though a horse had kicked out one eye

When Charlie died, his friends came around
To prepare his body for burial in the ground
Then they all jumped back in surprise
For Charlie had been a woman in disguise !

SANTA FE TRAIL

The Santa Fe Trail was key to America's southwest flow
It unlocked profitable trade with Mexico
In the Mexican War it was the U.S. Army's lifeline
Later helped gold rushers to California or Colorado mine

Before eighteen twenty-one Santa Fe was ruled by Spain
Contact with America they viewed with disdain
Would-be traders who came down the trail
Lost their goods and went to jail

The trip that established the trail now known so well
Was taken in eighteen twenty-one by William Becknell
Down to Santa Fe he led his mules loaded with packs
He traded his goods for silver dollars, stacks and stacks

That was just after Mexico got its independence
Later beginning in a town of that name is coincidence
From Independence, Missouri to Santa Fe, New Mexico
Eight hundred miles through Kansas and Colorado

The Mountain Branch over the Raton and Devil's Rock
Was one way traders could travel with their trading stock
Or Cimarron Cutoff, thru desert called Jornada by name
Jornada del Muerto, Journey of Death means the same

A typical trip took two months its end to attain
Four hundred oxen and thirty-six wagons in the train
It stretched for a mile along the trail
Forty men handled the whole detail

Death on the trail was a common event
Sometimes it happened by accident
Smallpox, typhoid, dysentery, and cholera, deadly facts
So too, Mexican, outlaw, Confederate, and Indian attacks

Against Indians, the army did try to protect
At different times, sixteen forts they did erect
To fight tribes Kiowa, Comanche, Apache, and Cheyenne
From forts such as Dodge, Riley, Union, and Mann

Carrying hardware, cotton , wool to Santa Fe
Sometimes they lost goods along the way
Rivers, wagon accidents, and Indians took a toll
If lucky, returning with furs, silver, and gold

After the Mexican War in eighteen forty-eight
The Santa Fe Trail was all in the United States
By the Treaty of Guadelupe Hildago
America now included New Mexico

The Santa Fe Trail was mainly a route for trade
Oregon and California Trails for settlers who stayed
The Santa Fe Trail was the oldest of the three
Also, the shortest one it happened to be

In sixty years of serving its historic roles
The Santa Fe Trail achieved its goals
The need for the trail ended one winter day
When the railroad reached the City of Santa Fe

The Railroaders

PICKING OUT THE ROUTE

Before the Civil War, they all agreed
A transcontinental railway was a need
But they just could not agree
Upon what the route should be

Long before the track-layers
They had to have the surveyors
The Secretary of War sent them out
To survey this and that route

The northern group left from St. Paul
Governor Stevens of Washington led them all
He said to expect no problem with snow
Even with his own people, his credibility was low

From St. Louis, Captain John Gunnison led a group
Missouri's Senator Benton let out a happy whoop
But Gunnison was killed by Paiutes in Utah
Which opponents called a fatal flaw

Lieutenant Whipple headed a survey southwest
From Arkansas to Los Angeles some said was best
Whipple made a multi-million dollar error in math
Causing people to say, too costly is this path

Jefferson Davis, Secretary of War during these dates
Soon to become President of the Confederate States
He always favored the southern route
To help give the South more clout

For all other alternatives to fail first was his hope
But he had to send out Lieutenants Parke and Pope
From northern Texas to San Diego
Was the southern way to go

Secretary Davis collected all the information
From these four surveys of the Western nation
And with his "unbiased" southern voice
Said the southern route was the best choice

Davis and cohorts had one embarrassing oversight
Which took an Act of Congress to set aright
The southern route ran through Mexico!
The Gadsden Purchase softened that blow

Because of all the regional uproar
No route was chosen until after the Civil War
Then President Lincoln made the decision
Putting an end to all the geographic division

Lincoln had asked Grenville Dodge his advice
A railroad builder, he didn't have to think twice
Follow the pioneer trail up the Missouri and Platte
Where the ground is mostly flat

Lincoln signed the order to start in Omaha
Dodge built the Union Pacific from there to Utah
To join with the Central Pacific from Sacramento
Which used Theodore Judah's path from years ago

Ironically, after all the fights and fears
Within the next twenty-five years
All the proposed routes were built
Crisscrossing the West like a crazy quilt

GOLDEN SPIKE
--The True Story of Promontory

At Promontory Point, so the story was told
They struck the final spike, made of gold
With this hammer blow, so terrific
The railroad ran from Atlantic to Pacific

But this account was not quite true
Promontory Point was not the venue
A peninsula jutting into the Great Salt Lake
Building bridges to it would be a mistake

Several miles north the event was held
At Promontory Summit, the crowd swelled
Hammering a golden spike, another mistake
Unless you want a golden pancake

So, in truth no golden spike was struck
Though they had two spikes of gold for luck
And one of silver for another toy
And one of gold, silver, and iron alloy

These four spikes played their roles
Being dropped into pre-drilled holes
(and hopefully soon were retrieved
before they could be thieved)

One iron spike was resting nearby
To be driven into the last railroad tie
But, alas, its fate was unfulfilled
The hammer wielders being unskilled

Iron spike and hammer, each wired
By telegraph, people would be inspired
When the hammer hit the spike
All America would hear the strike

Stanford of the Central Pacific first to swing
Then Durant of the Union Pacific his fling
They launched mighty blows just alike
But they both missed the iron spike

A telegraph operator sent the news anyway
America united by transcontinental railway!

SMOKE AND CINDERS

First, I was just a kid watchin' the trains go by
Then I was a wiper, which is a greaser and oiler
A switch-engine fireman and a road fireman, too
An engine watchman, keepin' water in the boiler

Now I wear a striped cap and red bandana
I'm the engineer in the four-dollar seat
I'm on the throttle and the whistle
Cities and towns on a schedule to meet

Everybody waves as the train goes by
They all look up to me
I'm runnin' far and fast
And I'm runnin' free

This locomotive weighs fifty tons
Fireman shovels coal into the firebox
Conductor in the train, two brakemen on top
Fifty miles an hour this train clocks

But we get boulders and buffaloes on the tracks
Wrecks, runaway trains, a break-in-two
Trees and grasshoppers piled in stacks
Sometimes, stoppin' is all I can do

Canyons, switchbacks, and steep grades
Tornadoes, blizzards, and deep snow
Washouts, falling bridges, missing rails
Indians, gunslingers, nowhere for us to go

I'm a railroader in the brotherhood
Today I got a straight run on a clear track
Pullin' coach, boxcar, flatcar, mail car
I don't need the brakemen to hold me back

Ten-wheel locomotive and the highball sign
I'm gonna turn this monster loose
Smoke and cinders are a flyin'
Hang on boys back there in the caboose!

AMERICA'S COMPASS

Chinese men crossed the Pacific
building from the west, as if possessed
Irish men crossed the Atlantic
building from the east with equal zest

In this race between the races
both developed the knack
under very harsh conditions
of laying down railroad track

Though the American Civil War
had just ended
many Yankees and Rebels
were still offended

What could not be joined north to south
by war cries
was now joined east to west
by railroad ties

TICKETS TO RIDE

With a bold, forward stride
    they all bought tickets to ride
Rich people bought tickets
    for an adventure to discover
Ordinary people bought tickets
    to get from one place to another
Poor immigrants bought tickets
    a new start in life to uncover

First class passengers
    were wined and dined
As the darkness descended
    their seats were reclined
Full of quail, oyster soup
    and mountain trout
With the warmth of the steam heat
    they soon passed out

From the train, ordinary passengers
    had to get down
When they had a ten-minute stop
    in a wayside town
They had hardly enough time
    for food and libation
Before the train whistled
    and pulled out of the station

Oppressed people from Europe
    and eastern American slums
Were treated by the railroad
    as if they were bums
On wooden benches
    packed like sardines
Immigrant cars soon
    smelled like latrines

They all got to the same spot
    clock on the same dot
The rich people well-rested
    and bursting with pride
Ordinary people saying
    thanks for the ride
Immigrants falling to the ground
    while some of them cried

Three classes of people,
    they all had tickets to ride

The Old, Old West

THE BONES OF DANIEL BOONE

For the last twenty years of his earthly toil
Daniel Boone lived in Missouri
For twenty-five more, reposed beneath its soil

Then one day came a delegation dressed in black
They had come from the Commonwealth of Kentucky
To take the bones of Daniel Boone back

After fifty years our thoughts are sounder
We know we forced him out back then
Now we realize that he was our founder

Now we are done with all those sour grapes
We know he brought our people over the mountains
Before, we thought we were descended from apes

Anyway, we come for the bones of our defectors
We want Daniel's and Rebecca's, too
We are the official Kentucky bone collectors

Maybe we have been a little slow to react
But we have a nice plot of land in Frankfort
And a special ceremony we'd like to enact

I rise here and now in Daniel's defense
In Missouri's gateway to the west
He and Rebecca chose their place of residence

Daniel had led the way to the western frontiers
From the very area to which Daniel moved
Lewis and Clark would depart in five years

Daniel Boone had carried the torch this far
Other Americans then took it from his grasp
And carried it toward the western star

While his bones you may take Eastward Ho!
Paying them the honor which they are due
Westward went his spirit long, long ago

BIRD WOMAN

Without the help of Bird Woman
Meriwether Lewis and William Clark
Would have been lost in the dark

She was guide, interpreter, and more
Sacajawea was her Shoshoni name
But Lewis and Clark got most of the fame

Up the Missouri River and beyond
She kept the expedition on the right track
All with her newborn baby on her back

From St. Louis to the Pacific Ocean
The expedition defined in great detail
The route that became the Oregon Trail

Bird Woman was her English name
The white settlers who followed behind
Followed in the light she had shined

MOUNTAIN MEN

In Europe, beaver hats were all the rage
Putting the beaver on America's center stage
After Lewis and Clark, fur trappers headed west
Beaver pelts were their primary quest

They became known as Mountain Men
Spending winters holed up in a den
In the wilderness many of them died
Some lived to be scout, explorer, guide

These men played an even greater role
In reaching America's western goal
Through rocks, deserts, and pines
Across unknown spaces they drew lines

Three of the best were good friends
Though their trails had different ends
Jim Bridger, Kit Carson, and Joe Walker
Kit the best known, Jim the biggest talker

Today, Joe Walker is not known as well
Though he had the most discoveries to tell
Through the Rockies, California, and Southwest
As pathfinder and explorer, maybe the best

Jim Bridger spent three years after one attack
With a Blackfoot arrowhead in his back
He showed the railroad, passes they could take
He said he discovered the Great Salt Lake

From Walker and Bridger, Kit Carson learned
Became the hero of dime novels people yearned
He helped John Fremont the Oregon Trail explore
Was an Army scout, and a general in the Civil War

These Mountain Men blazed the trail
For all who followed, lifted the veil
For the Old West of rip-roaring reputation
The Mountain Men layed the foundation

RENDEZVOUS

I'm ridin' this mule
And leadin' the one behind
Leavin' the rendezvous
Headin' back up the river

Summer's pushin' on
It'll take me a month or so
To get back up to beaver country
Goin' a little further north this year

Takin' the mules
I can pack in a lot more
Than I usually carry on my back
I'm travelin' heavy for sure

The Indian woman I traded
Was good company last winter
But I couldn't resist two mules
Even knowin' the feller was drunk

My problem once I get there
Is findin' some Indian
To take these mules off my hands
They'll be worthless over the winter

Right now though
I ain't walkin'
And I ain't carryin'
So I love these mules

I'm packin' in a lot of luxuries
Coffee, tobacco, tea, trinkets for tradin'
More than I ever took before
I got six new books, too

I ain't complainin' none
I give somethin' up
And I got somethin' back
We're all in the tradin' business

As usual, I got all my knives
Two pistols, and a big Hawken rifle
Powder, and a hundred pounds of lead
This time I got eight traps

Last spring I come down the river
With four hundred pounds of beaver pelt
I had to settle for the goin' rate
But I had a lot of money for a few days

I got drunk pretty quick
I'd been out of whiskey for quite a spell
A bunch of us old trapper friends
Started gamblin' like we was rich

A couple of weeks later
I woke up about noon
Half my money was gone
I put the rest in my clean pair of socks

We kept on drinkin' and singin'
And dancin' and howlin' at the moon
But I learned my lesson again
I kept better track of my money

We'd all been out in the wilds
Maybe saw ten Indians and two whites
We was ready to celebrate
And we sure the hell did!

But the summer was comin' to an end
So we had to buy new supplies
From the same company bought our furs
That's how the thing works out

Well, my money's almost gone
But I got a lot of supplies
Necessities for the wilderness
Trinkets for the Indians, too

When I get to where I'm goin'
I got to trade these mules for buffalo robes
Put one on bottom and one on top
You might live through the winter

Water in the river looks pretty low
Could be lack of rain
Could be the damn beavers
I'll find out soon enough

I'm lookin' for a hollowed out place
On a mountainside, near a river
And I need some flat spots, too
So I can scrape the beaver pelts

I'm pushin' up a little higher this year
'cause I know we all took a lot of beavers
Downstream last fall and spring
And they ain't there no more

But I don't want to get too far north
Them damn Blackfeet still hold a grudge
'cause Meriwether Lewis shot one of them
That must've been thirty years ago

I find somethin' like I'm lookin' for
Scout it all around for a mile or two
Dig a bit and move some rocks
Start makin' myself at home

My luck's good 'cause in less than a week
An Indian pokes his head up
Over the ridge on my left
He looks friendly enough

We talk a lot of sign language
He winds up with the mules
I get two buffalo robes, a tobacco pipe
And the hind quarter of a deer

I cut the deer up, roast some
Dry some out for jerky
Clear out my shallow cave
And arrange my buffalo hide bed

I won't stay in a deep cave
Too many bats, too many bears
A shallow one holds some heat
And keeps the rain off your head

Later the snow will come
And you can make a wall out of it
It helps keep the howlin' wind
And the pesky critters out

As the weather gets colder
The hides and furs get better
And I start trappin' faster
Beaver is the best to get

Men in Europe are wearin' beaver hats
I wade out into the freezin' water
Set my traps underneath the surface
So the trapped beavers will drown

I set all eight of my traps
In four different beaver ponds
A few days later, I collect the traps
Drag three beavers out of the water

Then I reset all the traps
In the two best ponds
Within the week I get nine more beavers
Then I start scrapin' the hides

I'm eatin' some fish
Shootin' a few critters
I'm at home here in the wilderness
In a big, beautiful valley

I'll keep on trappin' them beavers
Until the water freezes over
But I do switch a trap or two
To dry land for fox and ermine

Skinnin' out and scrapin'
Keeps me real busy
'til a blizzard hits my valley
I'm lucky to bring six traps in

My snow wall is halfway up
The mouth of my little cave
It's iced all over hard as a rock
I'll be holed up in here for a spell

I've got wood stacked up
All along the back wall
And a bunch of frozen meat to cook
I'll read a book when there's enough light

I've got over a hundred beaver pelts
Stacked up outside under the snow
Not many other animals, though
The blizzard's a little bit early

One good thing is the bears
They ought to start hibernatin' now
So I won't have to worry about
Being clawed to death until next spring

Days and nights get hard to tell apart
I keep a short path dug uphill
To get snow to melt for water
And another one downhill to my latrine

I think maybe a month has gone by
Now, there's a lot of sunshine
And I break out of my isolation
Down by the river I spy an elk

Here's my winter's supply of meat
I get my rifle and double-check it
One shot is all it takes
The echo causes some puffs of snow

Dress it out, cut it up, drag it uphill
The effort wears me out
After being holed up in the cave
But I get a fire goin' and meat roastin'

Durin' the long winter
I set a few traps for small animals
Not a lot of money in it
But it gives me somethin' to do

After a long winter, ice starts to melt
I almost froze to death settin' traps
I fell in the water, got to the cave somehow
Started a fire and shivered under the robes

Next mornin' I was still alive
I got the fire goin' again
Ate some hot meat and broth
And holed up in my cave all day

On the third day, I went out
And collected two beavers
And set four more traps
On the fourth day, I thawed out again

The weather got a mite warmer
But the water was still ice cold
And the beaver pelts were still full
My stack built up pretty high

Then spring started the melt
Up high in the mountains
And I worked on my boat
A big, wide canoe

I framed it and stretched birch bark over it
Got two paddles carved out
Put pine pitch on all the seams
And stored it in the cave

Sometime about May, I loaded her up
With almost three hundred beaver pelts
And down the river we come
Sometimes faster than I wanted to

In a few weeks I was back where I started
At the rendezvous, sellin' hides
Drinkin' whiskey, gamblin' my money away
Enjoyin' some of the female comforts, too

Women, mules, Injuns
Whiskey, icy water, sixty pound beavers
Holed up in a cave all winter
Cuttin' and scrapin' and fishin'

It sure takes a lot of work
To spend all that time by yourself
In the middle of nowhere
But it sure was my own choice

This year not as many beaver pelts
Not like the years gone by
Some trappers got less than a hundred
You can't get much supplies that way

Maybe I'll do this for another year
And then just keep on goin' downstream
Where there's more people than bears
And somethin' to eat besides coyotes

All the way down to St. Louis
Get the top prices for the hides
Then keep on goin' east somewhere
They'd say I'm runnin' from the bear

But they never even seen a grizzly
What the hell do I care?
I been beyond the end of civilization
Nobody east ever had that realization

Buck and Louie didn't make it back
Though they'd made it several times before
We know they put up a hell'va fight
Here's to you Buck and Louie!

Now we got all these tenderfoots here
We talk a lot here at the rendezvous
About what we seen and done
Most of us are goin' back up again

Where the hell's the jug I bought?
Where'd that tender woman go?
I'm callin' your bluff on this hand
Then I'm goin' back up the river

I'll see you all at the next rendezvous!

The West Today

OF ROCK AND WOOD

More than a mile and a half high
Reaching for a blue and white sky
For more than an epoch it has stood
A land of rock and wood

Steep mountains of enormous size
Encompassed overhead by the eagle's cries
Sturdy mountains made of solid rock
Enduring nature's calendar and clock

Aspen and pine climbing the mountainside
Stacks of wood, split for the fireside
Solid cabins made of logs of pine
A path of woodchips in a curving line

Horses, cattle, and cowboys that still ride
Hunters seeking a sight of deer or elk hide
Rising in the mist are ghosts from the past
Those whose time here didn't forever last

Hard-rock miners working the trace
The Ute Indians that they did displace
Tie-hackers with their saw and ax
Steam railroad men who left their tracks

In this land of rock and wood
At survival, you have to be very good
Man adapting to nature as best he can
Because nature does not adapt to man

WIDE-OPEN SPACES

West of Old Man River
There is no end of places
That offer wide-open spaces

God and nature are the rule
People don't make the West
Scarcity of people makes it best

There are some big cities
Where nature temporarily is tamed
Except quakes, floods, and flames

Forty miles into a small town
Maybe twenty houses on the way
Half of them not home today

You can see the dust blowing
Across prairies and plains
And see the coming of the rains

Blue skies with white clouds
Floating over the mountaintops
Far and wide a view that never stops

Mountains that are massive
Valleys that are vast
Endless plains that forever last

A world of giant size
Surrounding a tiny man
Watching for flashes in his pan

Acres measured in millions
A log cabin back in the pines
Near the shaft of the old mines

Rivers that run and run
Sand and sagebrush everywhere
Volcano cones, geysers in the air

A long road without a house
Past shrubs and aspen trees
Leaves quaking in the breeze

Big Dipper, Orion the Hunter
Deep, black, starry nights
One of our favorite sights

Wild animals, room to roam
Pronghorn, elk, and muley deer
Not enough people here to fear

Thunder and lightning enough
To set a man's soul free
Winds from here to eternity

THERE ARE STILL COWBOYS IN COLORADO

There are still cowboys in Colorado
    Takin' the cattle out on the free range
    Cuttin' the hay like a member of the grange
    Sleepin' wherever they can arrange

There are still cowboys in Colorado
    Who still will ride for the brand
    Here and there, still in great demand
    Up and down, ridin' over the rocky land

There are still cowboys in Colorado
    They still wear jeans and rugged attire
    They still drink coffee around the campfire
    Long before the midnight stars, they retire

There are still cowboys in Colorado
    Driftin' around from ranch to ranch
    Givin' their horse a drink from the branch
    Givin' their luck one more chance

There are still cowboys in Colorado
    Who keep a good gun by their side
    Who put a clean brand on the cow's hide
    Who still ride full of America's pride

Workin' from daybreak to night's shadow
There are still cowboys in Colorado

COWBOYS, FOREVER

We have ridden the Rocky Mountain trails
On the sorrel, the bay, and the roan
In a million acres of wilderness, all alone

Over rocks and streams, through the trees
We have ridden quarter horses galore
'til we can't sit in the saddle no more

Up the steep slopes and back down again
On the back of a brown, a gray, or a black
Wrangler and drag rider cuttin' no slack

We have faced down our inner fears
Faced up to the reality of lions and bears
Lost all our citified woes and cares

Watched the elk and deer herds grazing
Ranch hands mending the fence rails
Wranglers throwing all the hay bales

Jeeps off-road high above the timberline
Ridges and valleys and clouds far below
All the mountain majesty God can bestow

Cattle and horses running the rocky road
Never again to be the tenderfoots we were
We've seen the horns, and hoofs, and fur

Drifting in from the East, green as grass
Inside now, the West will leave us never
We are rough and ready cowboys, forever

Sources of Fact and Inspiration

MY STORY

I hope that you have enjoyed this book. Now that I have told the story of the old west, I want to tell you my own story as it relates to the west, old and new. I was born in southeast Missouri in 1939 on a cotton farm. As a kid I lived outdoors from morning until dark. We explored the countryside, and played a lot of cowboys and Indians, as kids did across America. We collected Indian arrowheads, which were all over the area. When we filled up a cigar box with arrowheads, we threw them away, and started collecting all over again. Now, I sure wish that I had saved them!

Later I learned much more about my Missouri heritage. As a child my Grandfather Ross emigrated from Tennessee in a covered wagon just after the Civil War ended. He was a pioneer farmer in southeast Missouri. Much later, and unknown to my Missouri ancestors, I learned that many of the Ross family already had left Tennessee and traveled on the Mormon Trail with Joseph Smith and Brigham Young in the 1840s. In Utah in 1861 my grandfather's cousin Melvin Ross married Julia Elizabeth Smith, the second cousin of Joseph Smith, the prophet and founder of the Mormon Church.

Missouri was my home for the first ten years of my life, and the gateway to the west. In my research for this book I learned more and more about the pivotal role Missouri played in so much of the history of the old west. I had known about Frank and Jesse James: my two oldest uncles were named Frank and Jesse. In retirement, my wife and I have visited the Meramec Caverns, which Jesse had used for a hideout, and toured the house in St. Joseph where Jesse was shot.

Also in St. Joseph, we toured the Pony Express Museum where the Pony Express started, visited Hannibal the boyhood home of Mark Twain, and had a flat tire in Sedalia the first railhead where the Texas cattle drives ended. We took our grandson Nicholas "Nico" Randlett up through the Gateway Arch in St. Louis, riding in little tram cars rattling like mining buckets. In Kansas City we attended the exhibit of artifacts from the steamboat *Arabia* sunken in the Missouri River, and covered under dirt for decades as the river had shifted course.

One thing which I hadn't known before was that Daniel Boone lived the last twenty years of his life in Missouri, and was buried there. Years ago I was fortunate to interview a descendant of Daniel Boone, who was named Daniel Boone! That encounter and my Missouri roots gave me the extra oomph to write the poem, "The Bones of Daniel Boone."

The other state that has given me deep feelings for the west and western history is Colorado, where I lived part-time for ten years on a guest ranch deep in the Rocky Mountains, mingling with ranchers and wranglers, cowboys and a few Indians. I was the ranch cook every day and the ranch poet once a week. On Friday evenings I read some of my poems to guests around the campfire, alternating sets with a cowboy singer. My wife and I have toured just about every nook and cranny of Colorado, such as spending the night in the historic Oxford House Hotel in Denver, climbing the ancient cliff dwellings at Mesa Verde, riding the old Durango-Silverton Railroad, and visiting the courthouse in Lake City where Alferd Packer, the mountain prospector cannibal , was brought to trial.

We have seen the mountains in all kinds of weather, gone hours off-road with our friend Joe Weber to see the unbelievable seas of wild flowers above Crested Butte, marveled at the golden aspen trees , the cities, the old mining towns, and the abandoned mineshafts. We have watched the herds of elk running wild, the muley deer, the pronghorn (antelope playing,) and watched the big coyote watching us, and rubbed the thick fur of the rogue mountain lion that had to be shot down from the top of a pine tree. We have ridden up and down on the wilderness mountain trails.

We have been fortunate to visit all of the western states except Alaska, brrrr! I have guided a horse around the cactus in the Arizona desert, fired a six gun there, seen the irrigation canals dug by the Hohokam, ancestors of the Papago and Pima tribes of Native Americans. I have visited the Gila River Reservation of the Pima. I have stared at Superstition Mountain, a place of lost treasure and troubled spirits.

In Montana the Crow guides gave us a tour of the Little Bighorn battlefield. We spoke with a descendant of Curly, one of Custer's scouts. In South Dakota there is still a protected herd of buffalo, but after we saw them, we ate a buffalo burger there, anyway. Damn white people! But they do have to cull the herd. In Oregon the Fort Clatsop replica celebrates the winter camp of Lewis and Clark. The cowtowns of Kansas sprang up as the trailhead for the railroad moved west from Sedalia, and Fort Dodge is one of those historic spots. In Colby, Kansas there is a reproduction of a sodbuster's house.

Texas. We spent a night in a stone cabin overlooking the Palo Duro Canyon, a treat of nature, but also the scene of a battle. We watched the participants set up for a big chile cook-off during one of our many stops in Amarillo, bought a bunch of western nightlights for the ranch and headed west. Inside the walls of the Alamo, we had an overwhelming feeling of the agony of the defenders who would perish there, including Jim Bowie and Davy Crockett.

Yes, I've been to Omaha, the eastern starting point for the transcontinental railroad, and to Sacramento, the western starting point, and to the Great Salt Lake, the place where the tracks joined. (Sacramento was also the western end of the Pony Express, which started in St. Joseph.) I drove the devil's highway 666 through the "Big Rez" of the Navajo nation in New Mexico.

Rodeos! As a young man I interviewed ranchers at the Southwestern Exposition and Fat Stock Show in Fort Worth. Then I attended their great rodeo. I like rodeos; they show us the old west and the west of today. And they bridge the gap! In Wyoming I bet a buck with my friends in the stands on the stagecoach races at Cheyenne's Frontier Days. In Gunnison, Colorado Cattlemen's Days brings the top-notch riders into town for a first-rate show. We were also visitors to where the rodeo began: Pendleton, Oregon.

Western Museums! Oklahoma City is the site of the National Cowboy and Western Heritage Museum, and of the wonderful Old West paintings and sculptures of Frederick Remington and Charles Russell. In Colorado Springs are enshrined the heroes of the rodeo at the Professional Rodeo Cowboys Association Museum. Cody, Wyoming is home to the Buffalo Bill Historical Center and gave us another look at the old west.

All of these travels and life experiences went into the creaton of this book, along with secondary research sources, some of which are listed in the following Bibliography. I hope that you have enjoyed this poetic documentary of The Old West. Happy trails to you, and thanks for listening!

Selected Bibliography

BIBLIOGRAPHY

The more than a hundred Louis L'Amour books of novels and short stories, and the more than a dozen Tony Hillerman novels set on the Navajo Reservation provided a lot of atmospheric background for the author.
All of the listings which follow are history documents.

BOOKS

Backus, Harriet Fish. <u>Tomboy Pride</u>. Boulder, Colorado: Pruett Publishing Company, 1969.

Brandon, William. <u>Indians</u>. Boston: Houghton Mifflin Company, 1961.

Hawley, Greg. <u>Treasure in a Cornfield</u>. Kansas City, Missouri: Paddle Wheel Publishing, 1998.

Hill, William E. The <u>Sante Fe Trail: Yesterday and Today</u>. Caldwell, Idaho, 1992.

Horan, James D. <u>The Great American West</u>. New York: Crown Publishers, Inc., 1959.

Lake, Stuart N. <u>Wyatt Earp: Frontier Marshal</u>. Boston: Houghton Mifflin, 1931.

Lamb, F. Bruce. <u>Kid Curry</u>. Boulder, Colorado: Johnson Publishing, 1991.

Mancini, Richard. <u>American Legends of the Wild West</u>. Philadelphia: Courage Books, 1992.

Osterwald, Doris B. <u>Cinders and Smoke</u>. Lakewood, Colorado: Western Guideways, Ltd, 1990.

BIBLIOGRAHY (Continued)

Oswalt, Wendell H. and Neely, Charlotte. <u>This Land Was Theirs</u>. Mountain View, California: Mayfield Publishing Company, 1996.

Reader's Digest Association, Inc. <u>Story of the Great American West</u>. Pleasantville, New York: The Reader's Digest Association, Inc., 1977.

Rinella, Steven. <u>American Buffalo</u>. New York: Spiegel & Grau, 2008.

Reasoner, James. <u>Draw: The Greatest Gunfights of the American West</u>. New York: Berkley Press, 2003.

Sandoz, Mari. <u>The Battle of the Little Bighorn</u>. Philadelphia: J.B. Lippincott Company, 1966.

Seagraves, Anne. <u>Soiled Doves: Prostitution in the Early West</u>. Hayden, Idaho: Wesanne Publications, 1994.

Settle, Raymond W. and Mary Lund Settle. <u>Saddles & Spurs</u>. Lincoln, Nebraska: University of Nebraska Press, 1955.

Smith, Robert Barr. <u>Tough Towns</u>. Guildford, Connecticut: TwoDot, 2007.

Snyder, Gerald S. <u>In the Footsteps of Lewis and Clark</u>. Washington, D.C.: National Geographic Society, 1970.

Sorg, Eric. <u>Buffalo Bill: Myth & Reality</u>. Sante Fe: Ancient City Press, 1998.

BIBLIOGRAPHY (Continued)

Time-Life Books. The First Americans. Alexandria, Virginia: Time-Life Books, 1992.

Underhill, Ruth M. Red Man's America. Chicago: The University of Chicago Press, 1971.

Weatherford, Jack. Indian Givers. New York: Crown Publishers, Inc., 1988.

BOOKLETS

Bancroft, Caroline. Silver Queen: The Fabulous Story of Baby Doe Tabor. Boulder, Colorado: Johnson Printing Company, 1955.

Churchill, E. Richard. Doc Holliday, Bat Masterson & Wyatt Earp: Their Colorado Careers. Montrose, Colorado: Western Reflections Publishing Co. 2001.

Great Mountain West Supply. Lawmen and Outlaws. Salt Lake City: Great Mountain West Supply, 1995.

Sammons, Loline. They Came to Powderhorn. Gunnison, Colorado: Wendell's Print Shop, 1981.

Steber, Rick. Gunfighters. Prineville, Oregon: Bonanza Publishing, 1998.

Steber, Rick. Miners. Prineville, Oregon: Bonanza Publishing, 1990.

BIBLIOGRAPHY (Continued)

THE OLD WEST: A MULTI-VOLUME SET OF BOOKS
Time-Life Books. Alexandria, Virginia: Time-Life Books, 1974 through 1980.

    The End of the Myth

    The Expressmen

    The Forty-Niners

    The Frontiersmen

    The Gamblers

    The Great Chiefs

    The Gunfighters

    The Indians

    The Mexican War

    The Pioneers

    The Railroaders

    The Rivermen

    The Soldiers

    The Spanish West

    The Texans

    The Trailblazers

    The Women

BIBLIOGRAPHY (Continued)

<u>WILD WEST</u> MAGAZINE.
   Leesburg, Virginia: Cowles History Group.

Banash, Stan (Tex.) "John Wesley Hardin Was Perhaps the Most Prolific and Fearless Killer in the Old West." August, 1996.

Bankes, James. "Wild Bill' Hickok." August, 1996.

Blackwood, Gary L. "Klondike Fever." August, 1996.

Brooke, Bob. "Wagon Tracks West." August, 1993.

Brown, Larry K. "The 'Hog Ranches' of Wyoming." December, 1995.

Cary, Diana Serra. "The 'California Diamond,' Little Lotta Crabtree, Rose to Fame in the Rough Gold Rush Country." June,1998.

Eherts, Walter. "Striking It Rich in Leadville." June, 1996.

Ernst, Paul D. "The Winnemucca Bank Holdup." June, 1998.

Everett, George. "Ex-Slave Mary Fields Felt at Home in Montana, Whether Working in a Convent or Managing a Mail Route." February, 1996.

Gilmore, Donald L. "Showdown at Northfield." August, 1996.

BIBLIOGRAPHY (Continued)

<u>WILD WEST</u> MAGAZINE.

Knudsen, Dean. "Forgotten Participants: Custer's Crow and Arikara ('Ree') Scouts at the Little Bighorn." June, 1996.

Mackessy, Mike P. "Texas Longhorns: A Short History." April, 1996.

Michno, Greg. "Guns of the Little Bighorn." June, 1998.

Niderost, Eric. "Sante Fe Trail Trade." August, 1996.

Paul, Lee. "The Alamo: 13 Days of Glory." February, 1996.

Peterson, Nancy M. "Captain Marsh: Master of the Missouri." December, 1995.

Reedstrom, E. Lisle. "6 Legendary Poker Hands." April, 1995.

Siegel, Nan. "Whether Cooking, Branding, Homesteading or Nursing, a Woman's Work in the West Was Seldom Done." December, 1993.

Smith, Robert Bart. "The West's Deadliest Dentist." April, 1994.

Zentner, Joseph L. "From a Valley Called Death." June, 1995.

SOURCES OF GRAPHICS

https://openclipart.org

http://jsmagic.net

http://oldwestdailyreader.com

http://www.wpclipart.com

Index of Poems

INDEX OF POEMS

	Page
The Pioneers	**1**
Headin' West	2
Sodbusters	3
Cattle Drive	4
Chuck Wagon Cook	6
Windmills	7
I'm Ridin' this Horse	8
A Hundred Miles Closer	10
The Old East	11
The Mormon Trail	12
Wyatt Earp	14
Gateway to the West	15
The Gunfighters	**17**
A Family Affair	19
Showdown at the O.K. Corral	20
Another Notch on His Gun	23
Wild Bill	24
Paying Their Respects	26
The Bible or the Gun	27
The Robbers	**29**
Bad Boys of Missouri	30
Me and Jesse	31
Jesse James' War	32
Kid Curry Breaks Even	34
They Pulled the Shades Down	36
Last Gang in the Old West	36
The Lawmen	**39**
Lynch Law	41
The Hanging Judge	42
Head Games	44
Cowtowns of Kansas	46
Switching Sides	48

	Page
Native Americans	**51**
Indian Names	53
Trading Post	54
Animal Spirits	55
Song of a Warrior	56
Medicine Man	57
Tribal Matchmaker	58
Indian Women	59
Trail of Tears	60
Treaties with the Indians	62
Indian Killers	63
Buffalo	64
End of the Trail	65
The Soldiers	**67**
Barbarians of the Border	68
Little Bighorn	70
The Buffalo Soldiers	72
Marcus Peepus	73
Fetterman's Last Stand	74
Devil in a Blue Coat	76
Roll Call	78
The Women	**81**
The Outlaw Girls	83
A Western Woman's Workday	84
Mrs. Custer's Last Stand	87
A Woman's Place	88
A Woman's Touch	**90**

INDEX OF POEMS (Continued)

	Page
The Prostitutes	**93**
Hats Off to the Ladies	95
All Aboard!	96
Pillow Names	97
Madams Galore	98
Daydreams and Nightmares	99
The Miners	**101**
Gold Fever	102
Flash in the Pan	104
Fairy Stars	105
Baby Doe	106
Boom and Bust	109
White Gold	110
Western Bonanza	110
The Gamblers	**113**
Indian Games	115
Gambling Fever	116
White Man Games	118
Preacher Brown	119
Dirty Dealing	120
Chinatown Games	122
. . . And So It Goes	123
The Spanish	**125**
El Dragón	126
La Corona y la Cruz	127
Californios	128
Feliz Navidad	129
El General Americano	130
Soldados Hermanos	131

	Page
The River Boaters	**133**
Ode to Mud	135
Up the Wild Missouri	136
Fire and Ice	137
Bad Day on Good Friday	138
A Hundred Years on the River	139
The Freight Haulers	**141**
Pony Express	142
Bullwhackers and Mule Skinners	143
Stagecoach	144
Charlie's Surprise	146
Sante Fe Trail	147
The Railroaders	**149**
Picking Out the Route	150
Golden Spike	152
Smoke and Cinders	154
America's Compass	155
Tickets to Ride	156
The Old, Old West	**159**
The Bones of Daniel Boone	160
Bird Woman	161
Mountain Men	162
Rendezvous	164
The West Today	**173**
Of Rock and Wood	175
Wide-open Spaces	176
There are Still Cowboys in Colorado	178
Cowboys, Forever	179

YOUR STORY

Dear Reader,

Please let me know your reaction to this book! You can reach me on Facebook. I'll be wearing my old cowboy hat!

My plans are for publishing three more books over the next few years or so.

If you loved this book, you can find out about the next one (which is not about the Old West.)

If you hated this book you can make sure to avoid the next one. Or, since the next one will be on a different topic, maybe you'll love the next one!

Anyway, either way, thanks for your feedback.

Sincerely yours,

Lindell Ross